THE JIM & DAWN MINETTE COLLECTION

edited by Gloria A. Staebler

Lithographie, LLC • Denver

Copyright © 2010

All Rights Reserved

Published in Denver, Colorado by Lithographie, LLC

Library of Congress Catalogue Number

ISBN 978-0-9790998-8-5

Designed by Gloria A. Staebler

Printed in the United States of America

Cover photo: LEGRANDITE (Cat. No. T0268), 2.5 cm wide
Ojuela Mine, Mapimí, Durango, Mexico
Dawn Minette-Cooper Collection; Jeff Scovil photo

This had always been our idea of the perfect specimen and became iconic of The Minette Collection when the collection was displayed in Springfield, Massachusetts. It was a gift from Derek Murray, from Tasmania, in January 1970. Derek had dinner with us on Christmas 1969, and Jim took him collecting at the mine in Boron. Derek left for Mapimi, getting there just after the marvelous find of legrandite. He sent this to us a year later along with a couple of other legrandite thumbnails. The specimen was pictured in Bancroft's *Gem and Crystal Treasures*. Dave Bunk and Dan and Diana Weinrich gifted the specimen back to Dawn after they purchased the collection.

We spent more than forty exciting years building our mineral collection; this is FOR OUR CHILDREN, who want to remember it.

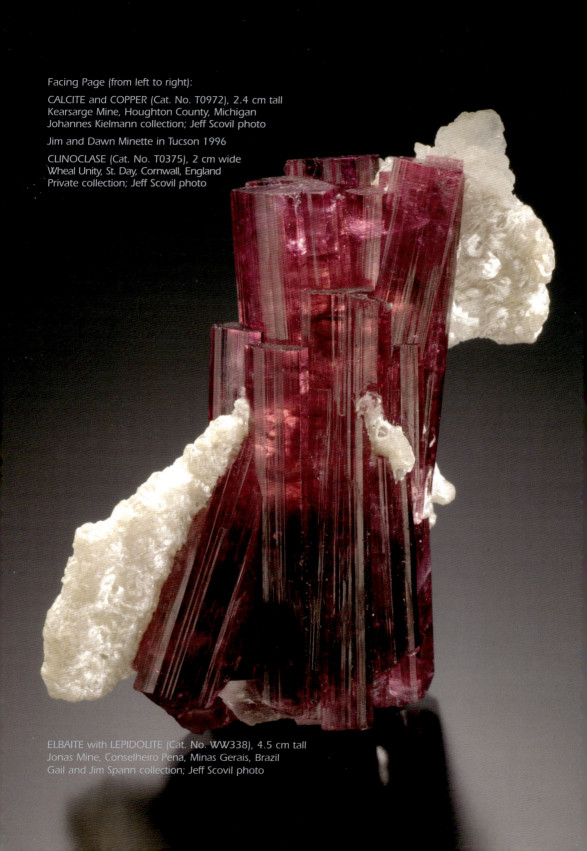

Facing Page (from left to right):

CALCITE and COPPER (Cat. No. T0972), 2.4 cm tall
Kearsarge Mine, Houghton County, Michigan
Johannes Kielmann collection; Jeff Scovil photo

Jim and Dawn Minette in Tucson 1996

CLINOCLASE (Cat. No. T0375), 2 cm wide
Wheal Unity, St. Day, Cornwall, England
Private collection; Jeff Scovil photo

ELBAITE with LEPIDOLITE (Cat. No. WW338), 4.5 cm tall
Jonas Mine, Conselheiro Pena, Minas Gerais, Brazil
Gail and Jim Spann collection; Jeff Scovil photo

CONTENTS

Acknowledgments   5
Essays and Images

SI AND ANN FRAZIER	Mineral Collection Catalogs	7
GLORIA A. STAEBLER	An American Dream	13
JAMES WELLMAN MINETTE	Funny How Things Happen	15
DAWN ELLEN MINETTE-COOPER	We Had Wasted No Time	23
ROCK CURRIER	Doggedly, Year after Year	31

The Collections

JAMES AND DAWN MINETTE	The Borates	37
R. PETER RICHARDS	The Smithsonites	79
GLORIA A. STAEBLER	The Thumbnails	131
PAUL W. POHWAT	The Mistresses	159

Springfield 2002   211
Full Circle   215
Works   216
Index   217

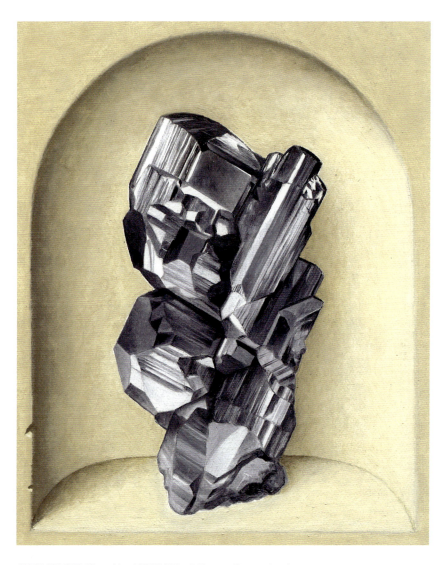

STEPHANITE (Cat. No. WW335), 4.5 cm all, repaired
Proaño Mine, Fresnillo, Zacatecas, Mexico
Wendell Wilson painting

ACKNOWLEDGMENTS

From Dawn Minette-Cooper and the Minette Family

We would like to thank Dave Bunk and Dan and Diana Weinrich for agreeing that we should publish a book about the Minette mineral collection. We would also like to thank Dave Bunk for insisting that we have Gloria Staebler edit and publish the book. She and her assistant Maya Strausberg spent many hours on the project, and it wouldn't be the same without them.

Jeff Scovil began taking pictures of our collection after he started mineral photography. Thanks to him (and to John Smolski and Jesse La Plante), the photographs are the stars of the book. We would like to likewise thank all of the people who contributed photographs and stories to round out parts of the tale, especially Si and Ann Frazier and Rock Currier. Si and Ann were mineral dealers we respected for their knowledge, and they provided us with good specimens from time to time, most notably our large alamosite. Rock has been a good friend and friendly collecting rival from the early days when we all worked for U.S. Borax in Boron. He and Jim often vied for the same minerals and did a lot of trading through the years.

Wendell Wilson made a beautiful oil painting of our stephanite from the Proaño Mine in Fresnillo, Mexico, and Fred Wilda did lovely paintings of our Mexican legrandite and Bolivian vivianite specimens that are featured in the book.

Special thanks to Marty Zinn and Dave Bunk for their help with the memorial exhibit at Springfield in 2002; the show would never have gone on without them. We have had help and encouragement from many of our friends, including Les and Paula Presmyk, Wayne and Dona Leicht, Bill and Elizabeth Moller, C. Carter Rich, and others. Many fine people and enduring friends are part of the mineral collecting community.

From Gloria Staebler and Lithographie

We wish to extend our gratitude to those individuals who assisted in the editorial process or provided background information in pictured specimens: Wendell Wilson, Dan Weinrich, Bill Besse, Elise Skalwold, Nancy Stevens, Si and Ann Frazier, Rock Currier, Pete Richards, Guenther Neumeier, Jesse La Plante, Terry Wallace, Peter Megaw, Demetrius Pohl, John Watson, Bill Dameron, Carolyn Manchester, Carl Acosta, Michael Minette, Garth Minette, Paul Harter, Sheila Bigelow, Lavon Smith-Todt, John Smolski, Les Presmyk, and Bob Eveleth. Special thanks go out to Dave Bunk Minerals, Weinrich, Inc., and the Minette Family Trust for their support of this project.

Finally I would like to thank Dawn Minette-Cooper, Jeff Scovil, Maya Strausberg, Hollie Rebaza, Mike Jensen, Paul Pohwat, and especially Dave Bunk for making this book a reality. Their talent and effort lightened my load and enriched this publication enormously.

A hand-colored plate (No. 94) of "Carbonate of Copper" reproduced from volume one of James Sowerby's *British Mineralogy* (1802–1817). This plate was taken from the five-volume set that Jim and Dawn Minette had in their library. Dave Bunk collection Jesse La Plante photo

MINERAL COLLECTION CATALOGS
an introduction by Si and Ann Frazier

Early Catalogs

Few, if any, of the world's early mineral collections have survived intact to the present day. To gain an appreciation for the types and natures of the specimens that early mineral collectors amassed, we are largely dependent on the few available books describing those collections. Without these books, we would have a very limited view of the specimens that were available at the time, the localities that were being collected, and the interests of collectors of that day.

Even for the most dedicated and energetic bibliophiles, old mineral catalogs are difficult to come by, a pity for those interested in the historical aspects of mining and mineral collecting and to whom every tidbit of information is of immense value. Of the catalogs that do exist, each is distinctive, reflecting the collector's personality, motivations, and opportunities. Over the years, we have had numerous chances to visit, via the written word, a number of old collections and collectors, and we cherish each of these opportunities.

Published catalogs of private mineral collections date, in the west, to that of one Johann Kentmann (1518–1574). He was born in Dresden, Germany, studied at Leipzig, then in Italy at Padua, Rome, and Bologna, receiving a degree in medicine and surgery in 1549. Kentmann worked as a medical doctor and wrote on botany, zoology, and mineralogy. In 1565, a catalog of Kentmann's mineral collection, *Nomenclaturae Rerum Fossilium, que in Misnia Praecipue, et in Alijs Regionibus Quoque Inveniuntur* (Nomenclature Regarding Things Dug Up, Especially in Miessen, and also Found in Other Regions) was published. "In it, Kentmann presents his … detailed inventory of the 1,608 mineral specimens in his own collection; 1,136 of them from Saxony; and 472 from specific foreign localities, … an extraordinary compilation to represent the first documented mineral collection in history" (Wilson 1994). This book is extremely rare. We have never seen a copy, nor even heard of anyone who has. In Wilson's article there is an illustration of Kentmann's mineral cabinet, but unfortunately all of the drawers are closed!

Our two-volume copy of *Catalog Methodique et Raisonne de la Collection des Fossiles de Mlle. Élénore de Raab* by Mr. De Born (1790), is in a contemporary binding and is a bit shelf-worn. It was not until many years after we acquired it that we realized only 70 examples had been printed, "pour ses amis ou correspondent." We do not know if the 70 included the beautiful four (!) volume leather-bound set housed in the Mineralogical Record Library (bigger type, better paper), which is bound better and in better condition than our set. Whether in two volumes or four, however, Mademoiselle de Raab remains eternally charming and fascinating. She even had some good mineral specimens. The value of our *Mlle. de Raab* lies in its rarity, its age, and in the fact that its more than 500 pages contain hidden jewels of mineral knowledge and lore, unique to this type of book. It is a privilege to visit this mysterious, virtually unknown lady and, at our leisure, browse her extensive collection. Interestingly, the *Mlle. de Raab* truly is a catalog: There are no color plates, line drawings, or any other illustrations in the book. It is strictly a list of her collection: mostly just species and locality, but some with a bit of description.

Jacques Louis de Bournon's 1813 catalog of his extensive collection, *Catalogue de la Collection Mineralogique du Comte* [Count] *de Bournon*, which he eventually sold to King Louis XVIII after the restoration of the Bourbon monarchy, was published in 1813 and is very rare. The collection "was preserved more or less intact in the French National Museum of Natural History and the College de France, having been divided between these two institutions in the year of [Bournon's] death" (Wilson 1994). The catalog came with a separate atlas containing 21 plates of idealized single-crystal drawings, which elicit our admiration. This catalog provides wonderful insight into the kind of collection a very dedicated and knowledgeable collector could put together during the generally horrible time between the beginning of the French Revolution and the end of the Napoleonic wars (roughly 1789–1815).

Jacques Louis Bournon (1751–1825) became intensely interested in minerals at an early age, no doubt encouraged by his father, who himself had assembled an extensive collection in the family home. De Bournon pursued his mineralogical studies throughout his youth. In 1789, the French Revolution broke out. After fighting with the anti-revolution forces in Germany, De Bournon fled to England, leaving everything behind. In England, he supported himself as a sort of consulting mineralogist, cataloging collections of various wealthy English aristocratic collectors, carrying on mineralogical research and an extensive correspondence. By the end of the hostilities and the restoration of the Bourbon King, Bournon had accumulated a superb collection. After returning to France, he sold his collection to the French King, who in turn hired Bournon to curate it.

Having a famous and competent mineralogist prepare a collection catalog has a tradition tracing back several centuries. Probably the most prolific of these catalogue authors is Jean Baptiste Louis Romé Delisle (1736–1790), to whom Wendell Wilson credits fourteen catalogs in his unique article "Romé Delisle and His Bibliography," a long chapter in *The Mineralogical Record's* landmark publication, *Mineral Books: Five Centuries of Mineralogical Literature* (1995), of fundamental importance for both mineral book and mineral collectors alike. Delisle came to mineralogy after a career as a military officer with service in India and other places in the Orient; in spite of a late start, he became, with the Abbé Haüy, one of two towering figures in eighteenth century mineralogy. One of the most important mineralogy books of the eighteenth century is his four volume, second edition of the 1783 *Cristallographie*.

Ironically, although Romé Delisle would seem, with the benefit of our more than two and a quarter centuries hindsight, to have been a most deserving prospect for election to the French Académie des Sciences he was denied admission ostensibly because he was a "mere scribbler of catalogs." Is it too late to protest?

Exotic Mineralogy by James Sowerby (1757–1822) is a quite famous and collectible work based on specimens from many collections, although a number may have belonged to Sowerby. He and his family had a private museum to which many people contributed. Larry Conklin (1995) in his article, "James Sowerby, His Publications and Collections," published in *Mineral Books*, notes that the "list of lenders and donors of specimens to Sowerby and his museum reads like a mineralogical 'Who's Who.'" Conklin cites William Babington (1757–1833); William H. Wollaston (1766–1828); Henry J. Brooke (1771–1857); Smithson Tennant (1761–1815); Jacques Louis, Count de Bournon (1751–1825); J. Henry Heuland (1778–1856); Adolarius J. Forster (1739–1806); Friedrich Stromeyer (1776–1835); and Christian G. Gmelin (1792–1835). All of these men have minerals named after them and are important figures in the history of mineralogy. Many other prominent people in the mineral world made specimens available to Sowerby, who was an accomplished artist with an exemplary reputation and who appears, with our two centuries of hindsight, to have been quite a congenial personality.

Exotic Mineralogy (1811–1813) was published, generally in two volumes, as a supplement to Sowerby's five-volume *British Mineralogy* (1802–1817). Two of the volumes focus on the rest of the world, which evidently in the eyes of an early nineteenth century Englishman was "exotic." *Exotic Mineralogy* appeared serially between 1811 and 1820. It contains 167 colored and 1 uncolored plates. To be sure, for collectors to have had a specimen included in this very important (then and now) work was a singular honor.

The mineral collection of Clarence S. Bement (1843–1923) was adjudged by Frederick Canfield (1923) as "the finest private collection of minerals ever made. It is the best public collection in America, having but two rivals in the world. The collection contained some 16,000 specimens! In 1900, Bement sold the collection to J. Pierpont Morgan, who presented it to the American Museum of Natural History."

Larry Conklin in his fascinating 1986 book, *Notes and Comments on Letters to George F. Kunz: Correspondence from Various Sources, Including Clarence S. Bement with Facsimiles*, comments that prior to "the gift of the Bement collection by J. P. Morgan to the American Museum of Natural History there was no department of Mineralogy at that institution. Because the Bement collection was so large and so fine, a special department of mineralogy was established in 1901." Reportedly, all of the mineral specimens previously on display were put in storage and later mostly sold. All of the 12,300 specimens put on display were from the Bement collection.

In 1912, Louis Pope Gratacap, the newly installed curator of the newly installed Bement mineral collection, wrote *A Popular Guide to Minerals*, the last chapter of which covers the Bement collection. Bement, who had always been willing to pay top dollar for superior specimens, gains our admiration for being a "real" mineral collector in that he appreciated a broad range of mineral species, not just the spectacular or expensive ones or those that he was instructed or persuaded to buy. He was a knowledgeable collector, who was interested in mineralogy, and his collection includes "interesting" examples such as the quartz polymorph tridymite and other rare species that generally interest only a crushingly small percentage of mineral collectors. Bement dedicated himself and his fortune to seeking and acquiring the finest examples of each mineral species, as well as examples of the important varieties of each.

Gratacap's book covered the whole collection and was illustrated with 74 black and white photos of Bement's specimens. Most of the text of the book covers mineralogy in general, but the last chapter describes specific examples of each part of the Bement collection, including descriptions of examples of particular species. The result is a sort of checklist of the best specimens that a very knowledgeable and very rich person could strive for. What better stalking horse than the "finest private collection of minerals ever made"? A century later, Gratacap's book, written by an expert on the achievement of an accomplished and very knowledgeable collector, remains an invaluable resource.

Proper Documentation

An important part of any fine and valuable mineral collection is its documentation. It would seem to go without saying, but sadly, often very sadly, it does not. Mineral collecting is similar to other collecting fields: stamps, coins, art, antiques, antique firearms, chamber pots, etc. There are several differences, however. The most significant is that, at least in theory, mineral specimens are strictly products of nature; thus rather than identifying the artist or culture that created an object, mineral collectors are concerned with exactly where a given specimen was found, and if possible, when and by whom. Many mineral collectors are likewise interested in the history that a specimen survived following its recovery, as well as something of the locality that produced it. All too frequently, however, little or none of this information is kept. Having spent most of a lifetime involved in the mineral specimen trade, we have strong feelings about keeping accurate and detailed records about all aspects of collectible mineral specimens. A specimen without a label may well be regarded as useless, but with adequate labels and descriptions, all things are possible, including fruitful deaccession; inclusion in useful, attractive, and well-documented collection catalogs and books; and admission into other fine collections or museum displays.

Increasingly, collectors are keeping and protecting labels with detailed locality information, a responsibility that many collectors and even museums have shirked in the past. Indeed, any record of a collection, whether in the form of 3-by-5 cards, photographs, or a hand-written manuscript is of value to contemporary and future collectors and historians. The technology around computers and desktop publishing, however, offers great prospects for avoiding the terrible fates that have befallen many collections and, incidentally, adds a new and very agreeable dimension to mineral collecting.

We have an old friend from Europe who is very interested in agates and jaspers, particularly those from the Pacific Northwest. He has the best and most comprehensive collection of them that we know of. This expert-collector has several daughters, who are not at all into rocks, and he would like to insure that they know what he has. The result is a file of digital photos of each specimen with information about the occurrence, deposit, and what is special about that particular piece. He has done everything possible to ensure that his agate and jasper cabs along with the experience, knowledge, and expertise that assembled them will long outlive him and have the potential to benefit many generations of future collectors and will enhance, if not ensure, the financial security of his daughters.

This aspect of contemporary standards is, to our minds, better than older ones. Collectors, especially those seeking better quality specimens, are demanding careful and detailed locality information on mineral specimen labels. For a variety of reasons, mostly toward the less than conscientious end of the spectrum, the impulse to be vague, or even to obfuscate is somewhat pronounced among certain dealers and collectors. Collectors who are apathetic about detailed information may become convinced to seek out such information if they realize that their collections are more valuable if their curatorial obligations are taken seriously.

Contemporary Collection Catalogs

Presently, there is a plethora of books that document private mineral collections or parts of collections. To our minds this phenomena started with two books: *Precious Stones and Other Crystals* by Rudolph Metz (1964) and *The World's Finest Minerals and Crystals* by Peter Bancroft (1973). Neither book covers a single collection; instead, they spotlighted individual specimens that should receive recognition for their beauty, aesthetic appearance, and in some cases rarity. We have been both contributors to and consumers of the fruits of this trend, for which we are grateful because this genre of books ensures that the values expressed by our modern, documented collections are saved for posterity, even after the inevitable divvying up of the collections and the passings of the collectors themselves.

Recent years have seen revolutionary changes in the technology of bookmaking. Digital photography and digital printing make the inclusion of high quality color illustrations fiscally tolerable in a modern book. For a book describing a mineral collection, professional-quality photographs can certainly be extraordinarily informative and useful beyond its possible value in aiding the sale of the book, assuming the photography, printing, and descriptions are honestly and competently done.

What many have come to regard as "vanity books" have made superlative use of the new advances in photography and printing. These books record for posterity the current tastes in mineral specimens, among mostly affluent collectors. We welcome this infusion of "eye candy," which will one day serve as touchstone for future collectors who are interested in the mineral collecting values of the early twenty-first century.

But to accurately depict the values of our era, the permanent record should include documentation of a broad range of collections, including those of the less affluent but equally serious collectors. Contemporary mineral collectors are a diverse group. They can be born of any socioeconomic and cultural background; their collections reflect their unique perspective and experience. Fine and important collections can potentially gather on the shelves of anyone who commits resources—time, knowledge, or money—to the collection's development. To provide future collectors with an accurate sense of today's array of mineral collectors and collections, we are well advised to document the medley.

Another hand-colored plate (No. 115), this one of "Rock Crystal," reproduced from volume two of James Sowerby's *British Mineralogy* (1802–1817). The plate was taken from the five-volume set that Jim and Dawn Minette had in their library.
Dave Bunk collection
Jesse La Plante photo

AN AMERICAN DREAM
a preface by Gloria A. Staebler

As a publisher of mineral-related monographs and books, I am frequently approached by collectors with suggestions for new books. They sometimes suggest a locality, other times a history, mineral species or variety, while most book suggestions involve immortalizing a collector and/or collection in the form of a book. With a single exception, I have shied away from books focusing on private collections. So when Dave Bunk approached me in 2007 to publish a book on Jim and Dawn Minette's collection, I was reluctant to accept the project.

At the same time, however, I was intrigued. His vision was to document the collection of a "normal" couple. His hope was, in part, to empower mineral collectors who were feeling marginalized and priced out of the market. Dave viewed the Minettes as serious collectors, having thoughtfully put together a meaningful, coherent collection. The collection was being broken up, but perhaps the best of it could be permanently held together in the form of a book. The plan was for the book to go press after the collection had sold so that it could not be mistaken for a sales catalog, but would instead be a tribute to the collection and its creators.

Dave assured me that I would have control over the publication, but that Dave Bunk Minerals, Dan and Diana Weinrich, and the Minette family wanted to purchase a large percentage of the press run for free distribution to the collecting community. In October 2007, I traveled to Denver to look at the collection. After a second tour of the smithsonite flats, then seeing the oft-used sleeping bags flung across a high shelf in the garage of the Minettes' very "normal" home, I was sold on the idea.

Modern mineral collectors are a diverse lot, coming from all walks of life. Thinking about the Minettes, I wondered whether in Bement or Sowerby's time, some other mine manager somewhere had taken an interest in minerals and built a collection which, undocumented, had drifted into obscurity. I thought it would be interesting to publish a book on a dedicated collector whose lifestyle and social status were representative of the larger collector population.

I went several times through the nearly 2,000 specimens in the Minettes' collection and began to talk with other collectors about the subcollections and about Jim and Dawn. What started to emerge was a picture of a hardworking middle-class family whose American Dream was centered on their mineral collection, and in building it, they had raised the bar for other collectors. While I have been assured numerous times that Jim Minette was no saint, the purpose of this publication has never been to canonize the Minettes; it has been to present who they were, what they did, how they did it, and why it is meaningful.

In all, I interviewed nearly one hundred people: family members, friends, coworkers, neighbors, and of course, fellow mineral collectors, and dealers. Descriptors for Jim ran along the lines of "driven," "focused," "horse trader," "hardworking," and "lucky."

Jim was a mentor to many collectors in the community including Bill Dameron, Joel Bartsch, and Sheila Bigelow. To others, he was a competitor. He was not always perceived as being aboveboard or fair, but Jim was revered as a knowledgeable and intelligent collector. He and Dawn were generous hosts to the hundreds of visitors who came through Boron to see them and their collection. Visitors recall that Jim could be a prankster and noted that he was an excellent provider.

Dawn was a strong and supportive partner, adept at marrying strength and softness to get things done, while remaining ever the lady. She and Jim built the collection together; they conferred on most decisions. And though Dawn created the appearance of standing behind her husband, she shared Jim's passion for minerals, if not his obsession. Dawn, it would seem, brought a touch of balance to the team.

Jim and Dawn, like us all, had strengths and weaknesses; in short, they were human. For me, that is exactly what makes this book about their collection appealing and what makes emulating them and improving on their model possible. Jim brought all of himself—talents and flaws—to the table, building and documenting a fine mineral collection, which reflects the evolution of the mineral market over the nearly four decades during which he and Dawn were active.

We have had occasional opportunities to see in print what money could buy in the various eras of mineral collecting history. Here is an opportunity to see the kind of mineral collection that knowledge, commitment, hard work, and a whole lot of horse trading could obtain during the last half of the twentieth century.

WULFENITE (Cat. No. WW264)
6 cm wide
Helena Mine, Črna, Mežica, Slovenia
Gail and Jim Spann collection
Jeff Scovil photo

James Wellman Minette standing in front of his parents' Clear Lake, Iowa home on the day of his high school graduation in 1954

FUNNY HOW THINGS HAPPEN
a biographical essay by James Wellman Minette (1936-2002)

Life at Home

My earliest memory is of our family taking its first vacation in 1941 or 1942. My folks did not own a car, but my grandfather Frank Minette had just bought a new 1941 Chevrolet sedan, dark blue. My folks borrowed the car, and we drove up along the Minnesota coast of Lake Superior. I remember crawling around in the big rocks at a state park, quite a thrill as Clear Lake was not rich in similar conditions.

My home life was fairly conservative. Mother taught piano. She was a McPhail School of Music graduate and had performed solo concerts in Minneapolis. She taught music at a school in Coffeyville, Kansas. She used to laugh about the silly antiliquor songs she had to teach. After a year or so of that, she moved back to Minneapolis and taught music at a Catholic school. She later became rather anti-Catholic, mostly because of Dad's Catholic family.

My father was a quiet, nonassertive person. He would do anything to help, but a salesman he was not. The "salesman" at People's Gas and Electric (they sold heaters, refrigerators, washers, etc. in those days) where Dad worked was a man named Yeager. His son Allen was like him: loud-mouthed, assertive, bullyish. He was in my scout troop and constantly making Dad's (our scout master's) life miserable. On one camping trip, he overdid it. Coming home, the last few miles was through heavy rain, and the tarp on top of the car carrier was filled with water. When we arrived, Dad carefully parked the car with a slight slope to the passenger's side. He casually asked Allen to go to the other side of the car and undo the straps. When Allen got there, Dad lifted up the tarp and dumped a big load of water on Allen. We all laughed like crazy. Dad pretended concern, but I saw the grin when his back was to Allen. Allen wasn't much trouble to Dad after that. I was proud of Dad over that one.

Mother and father made an odd couple in ways. Mother was domineering, Dad henpecked. Dad was a good, solid, dependable worker with little ambition. His education was two years of electrical trade school. Mother tended to feel superior because she had a full college education: a master's degree in music. Actually with two years' education beyond high school, Austin, my father, was better educated than most people of the time.

My folks were neither poor nor well-to-do. Dad did have a job throughout the Great Depression, and they managed to build a house in the midst of it. The shell was put up by a contractor, and Dad did most of the interior work. This was a slow process, as they finished things as money was available.

Money was always tight, so there was much more reliance on homemade toys for Christmas than store-bought things. Some specific things I remember included an airplane and a cannon. The airplane was about 15 inches wide and long. The body was carved from a solid block of 4-by-4, with

Jim's parents regularly competed in the Clear Lake Chamber of Commerce's annual Christmas decoration contest. They won the top prize several times. Photo circa mid-1950s

overhead wings. It was painted silver. The propeller was driven by long rubber bands in a drill hole the length of the body. Cut from a solid block of wood, it did not fly.

Another Christmas, Dad made me a Civil War cannon mounted on a homemade caisson with small red wagon wheels for the wheels. Dad had found the iron cannon under the floor of a summer house on the North Shore of Clear Lake when he was doing some electrical work. He cleaned it up, repainted it, and I had a neat toy. The cannon was probably an old starter cannon for the boat races on Clear Lake. Years later, my sons Mike and David rebuilt the carriage and shot the thing. David took it across the street, loaded it up with black powder, and promptly blew it off the old carriage. I think that is when the new carriage was built.

Every Christmas, my folks went all out on decorating the outside of the house. In Clear Lake, competition was fierce for the $25 to $50 awarded by the Chamber of Commerce for the best decorations. My folks won the prize several times. I remember the plywood cutouts Dad made. There were roughly 3- to 4-foot-tall figures such as wise men on camels, a big star, and a crèche that were mounted on the fence, painted white, and lit in blue and white lights. Across the roof and fireplace ran a Santa, sleigh, and reindeer, also lit in blue and white. They also lit a pine tree in the front yard until it grew too big.

Mother was very competitive, and when she didn't win in any year, we would hear sharp comments for the next two months. One gripe she heard from others was that we had an advantage with Dad working for People's Gas and Electric, and we got free power. Not so, but Dad probably did get a discount on lights.

At any rate, if you wonder where I got my competitiveness in minerals, it may be genetic. I was a collector, pure and simple. Grandpa Frank Minette collected stamps, mostly American. His pride and joy was a late 1890s inverted center 10-cent revenue stamp he found on a document while working as an accountant at a lumber company in Superior, Wisconsin. He also built a rather good overall American collection. He had the "collector gene." Dad did not; I did.

I started with stamps, added matchbook covers, and dabbled in coins. Stamps were my real love, and while I collected everything, Germany became a specialty. A German couple, Bill and Hedy Burkhardt, ran the local Clear Lake Bakery. Mrs. Burkhardt helped dozens of people in post-war

Germany when they were starving. So she got lots of mail and pleas from both East and West Germany. She gave me all the envelopes and stamps. Years later when I traded off the stamps for minerals, I kept most of the envelopes, and some are rather valuable.

I'm always amused at how people find the nation's morals going to pot. In our class (in a straight-laced Iowa town in a conservative area and era), the beauty queen had to drop out of school as her situation became obvious. The handsome English teacher married a senior girl in her senior year, the Speech teacher was gay (I now realize), and one 14-year-old never got to high school; rather reform school for rape. I think little really changes in the world, only the degree, perception, recognition, and acceptance of it.

And, yes, we had a few black sheep in our family. One of Mother's sisters had several children, before getting married (and that was in early 1900s). Also the husband of one of Mother's sisters spent a little time in Leavenworth. Seems he was a bootlegger. What does all of this mean? We were probably a normal family.

High School Years

I started high school in 1950 in Clear Lake, Iowa. My freshman year was pretty active. I took the usual college goal courses: Math, English, Social Studies, and Wood Shop. The one year of wood shop was no roaring success, but it did prove very helpful in later life owning a home, fixing things, and building display cases.

At the end of my freshman year, Mother rather bluntly told me to get a summer job. She suggested I try caddying. We had a nice nine-hole golf course in conjunction with a convention/dining/bar facility called the All Vets Social Center. It was run by a group of four veterans groups: VFW, American Legion, AmVets, and DAV. Caddying proved easy to get into and was mainly dependent on showing up regularly (seven days a week), taking every job, and being a good grunt. There were no such things as powered golf carts at that time; so caddies had lots of work.

As a caddy, I learned a lot about people and life. There was always the loud-mouthed slob with a huge bag and minimal or no tips. We became adept at avoiding that type, but I would take them, as money was money. The best man I had as a regular was a Jewish furniture store owner from Mason City. He always took a caddie, tipped well, had a small bag, was friendly, and best of all, asked for me. The only other golf course in the area was in Mason City, but it had an anti-Semitic policy; so every Jewish golfer played at All Vets. The same fellow later gave my folks a big discount on furniture when he found out who they were. I learned that Jews were just like everyone else: good, bad, and indifferent.

Probably the most lasting thing to come from that first summer job was an entrepreneurial bent. I found out you could sell lost golf balls. I became adept at finding lost balls in adjacent pastures, learned what balls could be sold for, the value of quality, how to dicker, etc. Back then a Titlist cost $1 new, and I could get 50 cents for an undamaged used one. I made as much selling balls as I did caddying. One day the local farmer let his cattle into an untouched field next to the course. The cows promptly ate the foot-high camouflage grass and exposed dozens of balls. JACKPOT! During my second summer caddying, we had a major rain, with lakes all over the course. That proved to be a bonanza when the water dropped and all the past month's balls were uncovered. Clear Lake had a lot of duffers.

During my junior year, I managed to run for and become class president. Somewhere that year, I was hired as janitor-dishwasher at the All Vets Club. This job opened a whole new world of experience. The dishwasher job was about 30 hours per week, at seventy cents an hour. By this time I could drive, and my folks let me use our '48 Nash Bathtub provided it was just to work. The All

Vets Club was located on the north side of the lake, three to four miles from home, so my folks could check the odometer and tell if I did more than go to and from work. (I really didn't.)

Iowa was a semi-dry state, with anything stronger than beer being sold only at state-owned liquor stores. However, in Clear Lake, a resort town, at least four clubs sold liquor by the drink, and All Vets was wide open. In fact there were slot machines stored in the attic from usage before my time. Working in this atmosphere was fun and very educational, and it did not make me a drunk. It did foster my ability to observe people, and made me a realist about life and people.

For my third summer, I worked inside at the club, only caddying when there wasn't enough work as a dishwasher. That summer, the club hosted the Iowa Ford Dealers convention—at least 500 people. We rented a tractor, a big stock water tank, and trailer. We filled it with ice and beer, and drove around the golf course handing out free beer to all the conventioneers. Don Sprat, Louis Bratz, and I had to stay there all night to guard the hundreds of cases of beer. We also were told to stash 25 cases of beer in the attic for the club's use later. We also each ended up with a case for our fathers (I didn't drink any). I later heard that Ford raised hell with the club when the beer account was off.

At the very end of the Ford convention, we were washing dishes for the final banquet when I got really sick. I woke up the next morning; the doctor came to the house (yes, to the house). He poked me a bit and diagnosed acute appendicitis. I went to the hospital in Mason City and had it removed.

I couldn't work while I was healing from complications from the surgery; so my folks decided we could go to Colorado on a camping trip. An important and seminal event in my life was a stop at the Colorado School of Mines in Golden, Colorado. We had been talking to my high school principal about possible scholarships, and he had pointed out that Mines gave one four-year full-tuition scholarship to each state, so checking out Mines made sense. My folks really needed the help, and somewhere along the line I must have liked what I saw. In my senior year, I applied for and got the scholarship, and my life was set. Funny how things happen.

At the end of August I went back to work and through the next school year I worked a full forty hours a week (nights and weekends) for between 75 cents and $1 per hour. My recreation was to get an extra-thick milk shake and go to a movie on payday Saturdays. My social life was nonexistent. I had become a bit of an introvert. The job was everything; I was saving for college.

During this period, the state had elected a new Attorney General on a clean-up-the-state platform and Clear Lake was a target. All of the other clubs in Clear Lake were either raided or got out of hard liquor. All Vets held a lot of votes but was not immune. My boss Bill Bastian, a fine boss incidentally, moved all the liquor out of the bar into a kitchen storeroom. I kept a tray filled with shot glasses next to the dishwasher. I would fill up the shot glasses and get rid of the bottle. The bartender came to the kitchen and mixed drinks from the shot glasses, one at a time. If I heard *anything* strange, I was supposed to dump the entire tray into the dishwasher.

One night a stranger came into the club, bought a drink, and then went to the pay phone. The only thing the bartender overheard was, "Be here in 15 minutes, it's all set." The bartender told Don and me. We threw all the cases of liquor into the back of the company pickup, drove it into the middle of the golf course, and walked back. In fifteen minutes, the biggest guru in the Veterans' groups walked into the club to greet the "stranger." They spent an hour trying to find where we had hidden the pickup. We never did get raided by the booze busters. Politicians knew not to rile Veterans' groups, which were powerful at that time.

Our high school class was actually pretty good. It was rated as highest overall to graduate from Clear Lake. I finished seventh out of sixty-nine, but had the highest Iowa Every Pupil Test score yet recorded in Iowa. Even so, I was a bit of a rebel, a nerd, and a loner. My last semester was less than best because I just wanted to be gone. I did get the usual awards: Bausch and Lomb Science Award, Honor Society, Mines Scholarship.

The day after graduation, I went to work and drank four double shots of whiskey. It was the first

I'd ever touched, and boy, did I get drunk. My boss came in at about 10 a.m., marched me back to the far poker room and told me to stay there till I sobered up. He never talked to me again about it. I never touched booze again, at least not in Iowa.

That summer, I negotiated my first contract for janitorial work. I was getting $1 per hour by that time. I told Dick instead of paying two people forty hours a week at $1 per hour, I would guarantee that the work would get done if he would pay me $1.25 per hour for sixty hours per week. He agreed, and I had more money for college. Our deal was probably illegal by a social do-gooder's standards and certainly by a brain-dead modern Democrat, but it didn't hurt me a bit.

All was not slave labor at the Vets Club. One day Dick told us all to show up at his house on the lake, and he treated us to a day of water skiing. I had a ball, but got horribly sunburned and could only wear shorts to work for the next few days. One bad thing did happen during that last summer. We had very heavy rains, and the club basement flooded. We had to muck it out afterwards, getting rid of everything including some old barrels half full of gunk, one with dried wax. I rolled the barrel of wax up the old wood stairs, and pulled a muscle in my back. It was sore, but after work we went swimming, and the cold water caused my back muscle to spasm. EXCRUCIATING PAIN! I went to the doctor, but there wasn't much they could do to help back then. My back gave me severe problems for the next 25 years, spasming whenever I lifted wrong, was under extreme tension, etc.

As summer wore on, I grew increasingly restive. I was ready to get out of Clear Lake and Iowa and get away from home. I'm sure that a lot of my going to Mines was an initial desire to get away and do something more adventurous with my life. So when my folks drove me out to Golden that September, I was ready for whatever life held.

The Colorado School of Mines (1954-1959)

I would be staying in Bradford Hall, a brand new dorm and the first one at the school. My folks seemed reluctant to leave me (typical for parents losing their only son) and I couldn't wait to be free (typical rebellious son).

Hazing was still very much in vogue at Mines. The day before school started, some sophomores came by and called us out of the dorm. Several of us ran out and started wrestling with the hazers. I was wrestling with one (not very mean-spirited) sophomore, and we fell over. I put out my arm, and we landed on my hand, breaking my left arm above the wrist. They took me to the hospital and had my wrist set and a cast put on. It may sound strange today in the era of blaming others for all your problems, but I took it almost as a badge of manhood.

One of the first freshmen I met was Gerald Van Sickle from some small town in southeastern Colorado. My first impression of him was of a slow, small town hick. I remember thinking, "If this is the competition, Mines can't be very hard." Three months later, I was struggling, and he was tutoring me in math. He became a full professor at MIT. So much for first impressions!

Freshman year was a time of breaking my old staid ways (threw a few memorable drunks), learning to live in a crowded dorm, and having to really knuckle down to studies. A broken left arm was no help, being left-handed. The Descriptive Geometry (drafting) professor said that he would take that into consideration on my drawings. Lesson number one came on my first test drawing: a "D" or an "F." I took it to the professor and reminded him of his promise. His reply was, "We can't give favors."

I struggled the first semester, but had good times too. Grade-wise, I squeaked by with a 2.0 (out of 4.0). Math and chemistry were my hardest subjects. I was carrying 21 semester hours, the norm at Mines. I did some dating, went to frat parties (but didn't join), and generally started a new life. My academic life was, as mentioned, hard. It was difficult partly because I was a small frog in a large pond, but also because Mines was just plain hard.

My second semester was the most difficult period of my college years. I moved in with a different roommate, continued lots of childish dorm tricks (but no worse than I got). We were all discovering a life of freedom from parental control. My grades that semester were poor (1.5 out of 4.0). I flunked chemistry and backed off from carrying a full normal load of hours. When I went home that summer I was low, really low. I took a tent and went up to Lime Creek and camped, speared carp, and just tried to be away from people. The folks drove up each evening. After three or four days, I went home.

I worked the first half of the summer for the power company as a helper on the power line crew. The folks took me up to Minneapolis, and we looked into geology/mining at the University of Minnesota. When I looked at the courses, it was obviously wimpy. Somewhere, I screwed up the courage to return for Plane Surveying at Mines the last half of the summer.

My second year at Mines was much better than the first. I took fewer hours (which condemned me to a five-year course, a very common event at Mines). My grades were up, and life was better. I had also moved out of the dorms and into a private apartment with the Cokleys on Ford Street. I stayed there until the last year when Dawn and I got married. They were good landlords, always helpful.

A Mentor

Sophomore year brought crystallography and Professor Paul Keating. When I saw my first box of natural crystals, I was hooked. Professor Keating saw my above-the-norm interest and moved to help. A life-long passion began. Keating was an excellent teacher—a great communicator, but one who did not suffer fools kindly. He could hit a student sleeping at the back of the classroom with a chalk-filled eraser without missing a word of his lecture. His tests were legendary. Once, he gave an exam with twenty specimens of sphalerite. Years later, I ran into a graduate who had taken that test. Everyone got the first three or four right, but no one lasted past five. They trusted their minds more than the mineral tests.

Another time Paul heard some students talking about all salt minerals being isometric, so he soaked all the crystals on the test in salt water the day before. Another time, he had a smart aleck student who had experience as a collector. The fellow told Paul he couldn't flunk him. His final exam was twenty white minerals. He flunked!

Paul could be equally generous. He had a student who was doing well in school in everything else, but had flunked mineralogy twice, where the third flunk would have him kicked out of school. When he saw the inevitable, he begged Paul to pass him, and promised never to have anything to do with mineralogy afterwards. Paul softened and passed him. Years later, Paul ran into the fellow. He was teaching mineralogy at the University of Alaska!

Paul confirmed a story about an incident, years earlier, when his wife was killed in a car accident. In the court testimony, one eyewitness said the car was red, another said it was black. So he had his next car painted black on one side and red on the other. His observation that eyewitnesses are frequently worthless is something I remembered. Later, I saw my own weaknesses on identification of faces during stressful periods such as strikes. Thank goodness for the advances in forensic science.

During semester break that year (over my January 20th birthday), I went with a few friends to Cripple Creek, Colorado. We camped out in an old powder magazine dug into the hillside. It was minus 10 degrees Fahrenheit that night. We found a bunch of the old Bank of Victor records in another abandoned powder magazine at the Elkton Mine. If I had all those old cancelled checks with famous signatures today, I'd be rich. I did save a gorgeous linen mine map of the Elkton Mine, which I later gave to a Mines professor. We walked down the road to the old Cresson Mine, which was working. They invited us in, and we got a full day's tour of the deep mine (to 3,000 feet/914 meters), the last mine working in the famed Cripple Creek District. My first real mine visit. I loved it!

The Climax Mine

I spent the summer between my second and third year working at the Climax Molybdenum Mine, at that time in its full glory. I lived in a dormitory with another newcomer, who was from Oklahoma. Climax hired about seventy mining/geology students every summer and brought a busload of recruits in each week from Oklahoma City (high turnover).

Work started with a multi-day safety training course, which was quite good. That was on the Phillipson Level, at about 11,200 feet above sea level. My first actual work was on the lower Storke Level, at about 10,500 feet. My first job was as a "whistle punk," which meant an assistant on the engine of the ore train. I ran the signal lights to the slusher operator loading ore cars, threw some switches, etc. We worked six days a week. Once one of the trains went too fast through the portal, a loaded car jumped the track, tore out some timbers, and caused a cave-in. We got an extra shift's pay by being trapped underground. I then got to run the slusher, loading cars. I screwed up the first three cars by overloading them, dropping the dipper in the car, etc. The boss bailed me out but made me shovel up the spills. Then I got the hang of it and did okay. Next, I got to run the train, and by squeezing in an extra trip, set a new production record. I ran just over the time limit and got an hour's overtime. After about the third time in a single week, the boss told us to knock it off. We knew we had stretched the rules and quit the extra trip. My wages when I started were $1.97 per hour and were raised to about $2.25 or so when I was working as a slusher operator. In this job, I frequently handled dynamite to shoot hang ups and break boulders.

Two months into the summer, the company decided to get away from contract mining for its development work. The miners had been abusing the contract system, and management had poorly administrated the contracts. The net result was that many miners were unhappy, and many quit. I transferred to the development crew as the pay was higher than on the production crew. It was here that I saw how weak management and unhappy workers could combine to create serious problems. I watched miners throw drill steel and bits behind timbers or into ore cars; I watched them break steel by forcing hydraulic jumbo booms into a bind; and I watched them just doing nothing. I was on graveyard shift, and it was cold if you weren't working. I worked to keep warm, and the miners threatened me for it. I backed off slightly but soon was working normally. This was the beginning of the life-long antipathy I have had for unions and poor management.

When I went on a mining crew, the idea was that I would stay all winter and earn enough money to continue college. Eventually though, I realized it was a trap. If I dropped out, it would only grow harder to return to school. So I went back.

The mine produced fine large pyrite crystals, some rhodochrosite crystals, and fluorite. One night on production crew, large pyrites started coming out of the ore passes. I got some, but another miner found one that barely fit into a lunch bucket. On the mining crew, I spent lunch hours climbing atop the timbers in a "talc slip," a white clay gouge that had sharp pyrites in it. I used a long piece of rebar to poke around and knock out a few crystals. I also got some rhodochrosite near the floor, but it was only in cleavages. I had neither the tools nor the experience to follow up on the rhodochrosite. This was the tenuous start to my collecting.

The summer at Climax was also a turning point for me. It was wet, cold, and miserable, but I loved it! Finally I was doing something adventurous and manly. I changed my major from Geology to Metal Mining, and never looked back. Mining and mineral collecting were now in my blood.

Dawn Ellen Hayford was about sixteen when she posed for this photo outside of her family's apartment in China Lake, California. Her mother and her grandmother made the skirt and blouse she is wearing.

WE HAD WASTED NO TIME
our lives in sum by Dawn Minette-Cooper

I was born and raised in California, beginning life in San Diego, where I lived with my mother, grandmother and sister until Grandmother's arthritis and my sister Tauby's asthma begged that we move to a drier climate. My mother was a civilian working for the United States Navy. She put in for a transfer, and just after my thirteenth birthday, we moved to the Naval Ordnance Test Station in the middle of the Mojave Desert—China Lake.

The China Lake facility takes its name from the nearby dry lake. There is no outflow of the water that accumulates there. Water escapes through evaporation or seepage, concentrating the minerals that it brought with it into the system. As for all of us, minerals, geography, and geology were the landscape of my young life, but in the stark contrasts of China Lake, I was perhaps more aware of it. I discovered rocks early and had a small collection when I was young.

The Kern County earthquake occurred while we were living on the base at China Lake. I was asleep early in the morning of July 21, 1952, when I was awakened by what I thought was Tauby bouncing on my bed. As I woke up, I realized that the ground was rumbling. The whole house was shaking and groaning, and the windows were rattling. The magnitude 7.3 quake did only minor damage in China Lake, but it destroyed many downtown buildings in Tehachapi, killing twelve people.

A month later, a magnitude 5.8 aftershock centered in Bakersfield destroyed parts of their downtown and killed two people. It was only the fifth strongest aftershock that followed the Kern County quake, but it caused considerable damage. According to the USGS, the damage resulted from the high-frequency shaking, the proximity of the epicenter to the city of Bakersfield, and the fact that buildings in town had already been weakened by numerous aftershocks. I was 15 years old and working in the office at the Navy Exchange that summer, and every so often, a sharp jolt would throw me against my desk. The ground quivered for more than a year. It was something I'll never forget.

I decided, when I was in high school, that I wanted to be a jewelry designer. I had heard that jewelry design began with the study of metallurgy, so I looked up the head of the Metallurgy Department on the base and learned that he had gone to the Colorado School of Mines. Mines was a pretty rough school at the time, and he tried to discourage me from going there, but my mind was made up. As a land grant school, Mines had to accept anyone, male or female, who met their steep requirements. They accepted me.

Arriving at Mines in the fall of 1955, I was one of only two freshman girls; in fact, we were the only two girls in the school. At Christmas, the other girl left, and I was the only female student at Mines for the second semester. When I left four years later, eleven women were attending the school.

The New Arrival
Proud parents Jim and Dawn Minette brought son Michael home to Boron after his birth in mid-November, 1959.

My years there were interesting: I learned to think like an engineer; I learned a good bit of geology; and I met Jim. Our paths probably crossed my sophomore year, in some of our classes. I know that by my junior year we were in several classes together, and we used to visit with each other in class. Jim was a student employee for Professor Paul Keating, the head the Mineralogy/Crystallography section of the Geology Department. Paul and I were well acquainted because I loved minerals and used to visit him in his office.

I often ran into Jim there. He and I would talk, but we didn't go out until the spring of my junior year, after Engineer's Day. Jim was doing a chemistry experiment in one of the labs on Engineer Day, and I took a picture of him. He later told me that he thought, "Ah ha, she's interested in me!" He asked me out. We went on a date every day that week, and at the end of the week, he sat me down on his lap and asked me to marry him. His proposal scared me almost to death, but I knew if I refused, I'd never get to know him. If I accepted, at least I'd get a chance to get better acquainted, and I could say no later, if I had to. I never changed my answer, and we were married two days after the Christmas of 1958. Thus began our forty-four-year-long joint mineral odyssey.

We were married during our senior year. After my first year, I had changed my field of study to geology, which was a better fit for me. I had to finish one more semester to get my degree, but I never did. By the time Jim graduated in May, I was pregnant. Jim had had a deferment from the draft while he was going to college, and we had expected him to have to go into the service when he graduated. But my getting pregnant changed the situation because the military wasn't taking fathers, not even expectant ones; so Jim began looking for a job. Jim went to work that spring at the Climax Molybdenum Mine in Climax, Colorado (elevation 11,360 feet/3,465 meters).

We didn't think I would do well at the higher elevation while I was pregnant because I had a tendency to black out if I got up suddenly while in Golden (elevation 5,674 feet/1,730 meters); so I went back to China Lake to stay with my mother. Neither of us had expected to be married from a distance; so Jim came to Southern California to look for a job. As luck would have it, U.S. Borax needed an engineer 65 miles south of China Lake in Boron, California, and Jim got the job. He started there August 27, 1959.

Mike was born in November of the same year. We had wasted no time. Jim and I were in the open pit collecting inderite and kurnakovite the day before he was born. Just after the open pit was started in 1957, the mineral collecting at Boron was wonderful. Mineral clubs were flourishing at that time and the Mojave Mineralogical Society (MMS) was very active. We joined the club when we arrived in Boron and were soon attending mineral shows all over southern California. The Mojave Mineralogical Society had great mineral shows, and people came from all over the area to attend the shows and the associated collecting trips to the mine dumps. Jim led field trips and was an auctioneer at the Mojave Mineralogical Society's auctions. On the auction block were specimens collected by U.S. Borax employees, who collected during their annual, company-sponsored trip into the underground workings.

In January 1960, U.S. Borax sent Jim to Shoshone, California, to run their Death Valley operations for three months. Mike and I went along, getting Mike's collecting education off to an early start: he slept in the portal of the Corkscrew Mine while Jim and I collected enough colemanite to pay the doctor for his delivery. Then it was back to Boron.

We spent a lot of time collecting in the open pit and in the old underground mines. We used to go underground and collect borax from the sumps, where water had gathered in the old workings. It was a lot of fun—I enjoyed old mines, and there were miles of stopes in the Jenifer, West Baker, and Baker Mines. We spent hours on the dumps making small rocks out of big ones in search of colemanite and ulexite. We had started to build our mineral collection by trading borates for other specimens.

Early in our collecting, we started trading by mail with collectors from a number of foreign countries. These trades were sometimes very successful. We met Demetrius Pohl in this manner. We spent many years trading with him while he lived in Australia and was traveling through Africa. Those first correspondences and trades formed the beginning of a long and enduring friendship.

I worked for a while for the company as a junior engineer (basically a cartographer), until David was born in 1962. I worked for another six months or so after David came along, and then I went into permanent retirement. By that time, we had already begun attending the Tucson and Trona mineral shows. We were mineral collectors!

Early on, U.S. Borax gave Jim a number of temporary assignments in the region, which opened new collecting opportunities for us. He spent three months on a dredging project at Searles Lake, California. While we were there, we collected halite and lovely, large hanksite crystals. Then we spent fifteen months in Carlsbad, New Mexico, at the company's potash mine. We found a lot of lovely potash and halite specimens in the Carlsbad mines. I enjoyed the underground mines near Carlsbad. They were clean and smelled a lot better than the average mine.

We did a lot of traveling and hunting for specimens while we were in New Mexico. Our trades with the museum at the School of Mines at Socorro, New Mexico, provided part of our fledgling smithsonite collection, as we acquired some unique specimens from them. We were regularly buying smithsonite from Tsumeb and other localities. In New Mexico, we had a mineral room with four large cases filled with minerals.

Jim was transferred back to Boron in 1965, but before reporting back, he and Father Luke McMillan, a friend, fellow mineral collector, and Catholic priest, took a two-week tour of Mexico, collecting and buying minerals as they went. We brought the mineral cases back from New Mexico with us and set up a mineral room in the middle bedroom of our new house.

In 1966, we won the American Federation of Mineral Societies (AFMS) Trophy for our thumbnails. Dick Bideaux, a previous AFMS thumbnail trophy winner, encouraged us to display. I don't think any of the specimens from that first award-winning case were in the collection when I sold it. Our tastes and collection had evolved during the time between this first award and our 1984/1985 award-winning cases.

On January 1, 1967, Jim became General Mine Foreman of the Boron open pit. Management turned out to be a field he loved. Our lives were peppered with a couple of frightening miners' strikes, most memorably in May of 1968 and June of 1974. For the most part, however, we were becoming entrenched in family and in mineral collecting. Jim was committed to his work at the mine, which provided a solid foundation for our lives.

Garth was born in Ridgecrest in 1969. He completed our family. At first, Garth shared the middle bedroom with the minerals, but we knew that was not going to work for long. We decided to enclose part of our back porch, and Jim went to work building our mineral room. He built three large cases consisting of glass display cases atop banks of wooden drawers.

Through the years, we hosted countless friends and mineral-collecting luminaries, who came through the area. Sharing the collection and a collecting trip to the mine or to another area locality were always on the agenda. Thumbnail collector Gerry Blair brought his two sons by for a visit. He wrote about the trip in his "One by One" column in *Gems and Minerals* (1966):

> *... We collected on the dumps and found some very good colemanite vugs. The glassy colemanite was enhanced by its association with amber spherules of calcite and we collected several fine T/N's. It seemed odd to me to be able to collect crystals while sitting in the warmth of a bright winter sun.*
>
> *To insure that I wouldn't get spoiled, Jim Minette and Bob Bohm gave me a tour underground and we inspected the tired workings of the old Baker Mine. In the sumps of this mine, we were able to collect fine yellow crystals of borax. Unfortunately, this borax has too much water to withstand the dry environment above ground and, after a period of exposure and a subsequent loss of water, it alters to chalky white tincalconite. It is still an attractive specimen even after alteration.*
>
> *Here is the way we collected. We drove underground and followed a maze of tunnels and cross-tunnels for several miles until we came to a spot about 300 feet down*

Familiar to the many mineral collectors who visited Jim and Dawn in Boron, the mineral room was built by Jim. The cabinets on the right were purchased and installed some years after the room was built. Jeff Scovil photo

where there was a pool of water. The borax crystals grow right in the water, which is highly saturated, of course, with borax. To collect, it is necessary to disrobe and immerse yourself in the chilly sump. Inasmuch as I was "company," Bob and Jim allowed me the honor of the bath and I soon found myself up to my chin in the slimy sump. While I collected, they assisted by standing on the bank shouting encouragement. As a matter of fact, Bob used my camera to record my labors and I now possess photographic documentation of my swim in more or less living color. Thanks a lot, Bob.

We traveled a good deal for Jim's job as well as to collect minerals. In March of 1971, Jim went on a Friends of Mineralogy/Smithsonian Institution-sponsored trip to the Pine Creek Tungsten Mine near Bishop, California, to collect laumontite. Then in 1982, he took part in another Smithsonian-sponsored trip, this time to collect axinite at the New Melones Dam Spillway in central California. Bill and Elizabeth Moller, Mary Fong, and James Walker were among that group.

Jim and I went to South Africa and Zambia in 1978 as part of a Rio Tinto mining conference. That was a great trip. Jim met Desmond Sacco in South Africa and traded borates with him for rhodochrosite, and we got to collect libethenite at the Mindola pit at the Rokana Mine in Kitwe, Zambia. In 1989, we took a side trip to New Zealand after a Rio Tinto mining conference, this time in Australia, and collected sulfur on carbonized logs.

Our travels were extensive, and, whatever their primary purpose, we invariably found a way to work collectors or collecting into our trips. Jim's favorite collecting spot was the Champion Mine in California's White Mountains. He made several trips there and found a number of good specimens, especially rutile and woodhouseite.

In 1984, we won the American Federation Trophy for our thumbnails at San Diego. We also won

Jim Minette, right, hands a laumontite specimen to Al McGinnis in the Pine Creek Mine near Bishop, California, in March 1971. The pair were part of a larger team taking part in a Friends of Mineralogy/Smithsonian Institution-sponsored field trip...

The Twenty Mule Team Museum in Boron, California, focuses on the history of the Boron area and of borax mining in Death Valley and Boron. Dawn curated the museum for fourteen years.

the trophy for the best case of minerals in the show and won a trophy for the best case of minerals from the California Federation of Mineralogical Societies region. Those competitions served as practice runs leading up to competing for and winning the 1985 McDole Trophy for our thumbnail collection. We were very proud of that win. In the space between the 1966 Federation Trophy and our winning the McDole Trophy, our idea of a fine thumbnail specimen had shifted. We were no longer looking for small pieces that would fit into a one-by-one-inch cube; we were looking for thumbnail *specimens*—aesthetic matrix pieces and associations.

We had hit our stride both as collectors and in our careers. Jim was Mine Manager when the Boron open pit was given the 1985 Sentinels of Safety Award for the safest open pit in the country. Jim was very proud of that award, particularly because he made sure that the mine dumps were always open to collectors when the heavy equipment wasn't running.

I got involved with the Twenty Mule Team Museum and embarked on a fourteen-year term as its curator/display developer. I designed the early displays, many of which are still there today. I set up systems to accept donations and catalog the artifacts. I developed an historical library containing pertinent stories and articles about Boron and the surrounding areas. The library was used by archeologists and historians. The museum included displays on early Boron and its residents, U.S. Borax (now Rio Tinto), our local Solar Plant, and Edwards Air Force Base. With the help of the Mojave Mineralogical Society, which had a beautiful case built, we installed a case of local minerals.

In 1991 after thirty-three years with U.S. Borax, Jim retired. He had been a member of the American Mining Congress' non-coal Safety Committee for 20 years and had testified before congressional committees in an effort to protect the mining industry from some of the more onerous laws proposed to restrict it. He was ready for some rest, Jim-style.

Jim spent a lot of time cutting and polishing ulexite for sale after he retired. We still got out collecting, although not quite as frequently. Jim also began to seek out and buy old collections to sell. One of our most notable purchases came in 1994 when we bought Willard Perkin's collection. After retiring, Jim took up fly-fishing and spent a good bit of his time up in the Sierras chasing trout. He also made fishing trips to Canada, Alaska, and Chile. Catch and release was important to Jim, a lifelong animal lover.

I make appliqué quilts and built a dollhouse, which I will have time to complete one of these days. I write reams of family history, make bead necklaces, and am an enthusiastic amateur photographer.

In January of 1997, our beloved son David died in an accident in his apartment in Salt Lake City, Utah. I will never forget our car breaking down in our rush to get to him on that horrible day, nor the warmth and depth of the friendship shown to us following our indescribable tragedy.

Jim died in January 2002, and with the help of Dave Bunk and Les Presmyk, I displayed the collection as a memorial to him at the show in Springfield in August of that year. Before Jim got sick, we had agreed with Marty Zinn that we would be the guest exhibitors at the show, and I'm sure that Jim was there in spirit. He always enjoyed a good mineral show.

Jim collecting ulexite from a seam in the shale above the main orebody in the open pit in Boron. Wolfgang Mueller photo

Upper left: Jim Minette and Vince Morgan looking at a borate specimen at the Lancaster Mineral Show in 1991. Dawn Minette photo
Upper right: Jim Minette in 1972, Rock Currier photo
Left: One of the loaders working in the open pit in Boron in 1973; Rock Currier photo

DOGGEDLY, YEAR AFTER YEAR
by Rock Currier

    I knew Jim Minette for perhaps forty years. We first met when I was working as an analytical technician in the chemical control laboratory at the borax mine in Boron, California. My boss was Vince Morgan, a great guy, who sort of got me hooked on minerals. He had fine examples of crystallized borates on the bookshelves in his office. I asked him how he "made those things," and he patiently explained that they formed naturally in the mine through the process of crystallization. He told me I could go out on the dump and collect some; so every few days, I would drag in some recently dug treasurers and show them to him. He would then show me what good specimens looked like, and I would throw away my finds and go dig some more.
    I started collecting at Boron, mostly on the dumps where the big trucks were dumping the waste rock from the open pit. There were two dumps: The least interesting was where they dumped the sedimentary reddish sandy overburden. The second was where they dumped the "blue mud" layer from the top of the borate deposit. That was the dump with the colemanite, ulexite, and other interesting minerals that were found above the crystallized borax. Borax, pure sodium borate, was the target for most of the mining at Boron. The stuff from the top of the deposit, the colemanite and the ulexite, were good boron ores; in fact, they had been the world's primary boron ores prior to the discovery of borax at Boron. The company kept the blue mud dumps containing the colemanite and ulexite separate against the future when the borax is exhausted. Those dumps will one day provide millions of tons of boron ore after the borax runs out.
    Borax is super easy to process: it only has to be dissolved in hot water and recrystallized as saleable material. Colemanite and ulexite have to be dissolved in acid first; so processing it is more time consuming and expensive. Colemanite and ulexite were what they were mining in Death Valley. Ulexite was mined from the floor of the valley and from some of the dry lakes in Nevada in the early days. Colemanite was the primary ore mined underground at Ryan in Death Valley and in other mines such as the Thompson Mine, which is well known for producing big colemanite crystals.
    In the underground workings at Boron, there were sumps where fine borax crystals could be found. The only way I could get there was to climb down one of the shafts in the middle of the night and collect, then carry my finds back up the couple hundred feet of ladders; so I really could not get all that much out of the mine. Some of the guys I knew, a few of whom later became friends, had a better plan. One of them got a summer job in the mine as a junior mining engineer/gofer and managed to snag one of the keys that opened the gate to the big portal in the open pit. With that open, we could drive a car or truck directly into the mine, where we had direct access to miles of underground workings, many of which could by reached by Jeep.
    So this guy and some of my future friends would drive into the pit in the middle of the night (with their lights off to avoid detection), open the portal, drive into the mine, and close the portal behind them. This part of the mine was not active and had been mostly abandoned or mothballed when the

open pit began production. They had all day to play around in the mine and collect all the borax they wanted. Had they left it at that, the game would perhaps have gone on much longer than it did.

The power to the mine had been left on, and the old electric locomotives that ran the old mine rail system underground were still functional. The lighting system still worked and there was power to the underground machine and repair shop. Some of my friends were railway buffs and learned how to charge the batteries of the old locomotives. They started playing choo-choo and rode the trains underground for hours. At the top of an incline, they found a functional winch that they could use to lower the train down an incline to a lower level so that they could ride around down there.

The problem was that this winch drew a lot of electricity and using it caused the mine's power demand to spike. The mine's electricity rate was based on peak loads, so management quickly became aware that unauthorized personnel were playing around in the mine because the activity kicked up the company's power bill. At least that's what I heard. In addition, these guys were carting out Jeep loads of borax crystals that they were selling for hundreds of dollars a load to various rock shops in southern California.

Jim Minette was a junior mining engineer at that time, and a little of his extra income came from trading borax crystals and other specimens from the mine. All of the "extra" borax that these guys were dumping onto the market was cutting into what Jim could get for his stuff. When management noticed the power spike in the mine, they had to crack down, and Jim was one of the crackers. A new padlock was placed on the mine portal in the pit, and padlocks were placed on the trapdoor gratings on the manways that gave access to the underground mine at the various shafts like the old Baker, Jennifer, and West Baker mines. I had been using the old Baker shaft to do my borax collecting, so Jim's padlock spelled the end of my borax collecting at Boron. That was how I met Jim Minette; needless to say, my first introduction to him was not pleasant.

I worked at Boron for about six months and soon had another job working with chemicals at a company in Los Angeles. I regularly returned to Boron on the weekends to scrounge what specimens I could from the dumps, but more importantly to tend my network of miners to see what specimens they had collected. Many of them collected specimens in the open pit during their normal shifts, and their finds were almost always much better than what could be collected on the dump. I would stop and see my old boss Vince Morgan and my friend Howard Pomtier, who was the drilling and blasting foreman.

I had heard that Jim Minette was a collector, so I started stopping by his place to see if he had found anything new. He and I were independently collecting at other localities when we got the chance; so right from the start, there was a rivalry to see who could get the best specimens. Jim had direct access to the mine, but I had my network of miners who didn't want to show him what they had because he was considered management—a suit—who might demand that they not waste company time collecting, which would cut down on the money that they could get from selling specimens on the side. As time passed, however, Jim and I became good friends. I would often spend Friday or Saturday nights at Jim and Dawn's house; I even brought a bed up for their mineral room that I would sleep on.

Early on, I bought the borate collection of Beth and Weldon Gordon, Brad van Scriver's mother and step-father. The Gordons had collected at Boron in the early days, when the open pit was just starting; they bought specimens from the miners as well. In the apartment building that they managed, they had set aside a whole apartment for the display of their collection. I got the whole thing for less than $2000. It consisted only of crystallized specimens from Boron; the specimens filled more than 100 seat cover boxes—about 300 flats. This single purchase put me far ahead of Jim in our rivalry to build the best borate collection. I even sold Jim some specimens from the collection, although as you might imagine, he was reluctant to buy specimens from his own mine.

A little later, I bought the collection of Howard Pomtier, putting me way ahead. But Jim kept pecking away, always managing to find something new in the mine, mostly the new flavors of colemanite, which were encountered during the normal mining process.

For about 15 months, Jim and Dawn moved to Carlsbad, New Mexico, where Jim worked in U.S. Borax's potash mine. The move put a crimp on his borate collecting, but he found a place in the potash mine where he could collect crystal clusters of sylvite (potassium chloride), which he used as fodder for his mineral trades. It also limited our visits because Carlsbad was a long way from Los Angeles. I did however visit them once while he was working there. Jim got me underground, and I got to collect sylvite clusters from an old stope that had been flooded with a saturated solution of potassium chloride from the mine. The fluid had evaporated, leaving behind the sylvite crystals. Soon after, Jim returned to Boron, got a promotion, and became one of the guys who was running the open pit. I moved back east for four years to work and chase other kinds of minerals.

I came to realize that many of the borate minerals do not do well in places with high humidity, like Los Angeles. Sodium borate minerals such as borax, kernite, and tincalconite degrade quickly, but even "stable" ones such as colemanite, kurnakovite, and inderite pick up some sort of coating, although that seems to be the extent of their instability. A few years after collecting a beautiful shiny colemanite specimen and bringing it back to Los Angeles, I would find that it had lost much of its brilliance. Similar specimens kept in a cool closet in Boron are affected to a much lesser extent. So I more or less stopped collecting minerals from the Boron and Death Valley borate deposits, but Jim kept on doggedly, year after year.

He got into good pockets of colemanite, kept a few very fine specimens for the collection, and took as much from the pocket as he could carry to trade or sell. He found a retired miner in Boron who had a few super fine inderite crystals, which were better than the ones that I had. He collected the high grade optical ulexite from the mine, carted it home, and would either sell it rough or cut it up into "TV rock," which always had a ready market. When U.S. Borax sent him to their properties in Death Valley, Jim would always seem to find specimens, sometimes quite nice ones. He talked his way into the Thompson Mine and managed to collect some of the best hydroboracite specimens ever found (see page 66), and they made excellent trade bait.

Years later, Jim and Dawn bought Vince Morgan's mineral collection, which contained a wealth of classic borate specimens. I told him at that point that I thought he finally had the best borate collection. He was the mine superintendent by that time and was making a lot more money, which allowed him to buy better specimens for the collection. He occasionally took me underground to collect borax or into the open pit to collect something he had just located. One time in the open pit, he called in a 10 yard front loader to dig a 10-by-50-foot trench in the bottom of the pit. That is the kind of collecting tool every field collector dreams of!

In my experience, borates are the least collectible class of mineral specimens, probably because collectors think they decompose and fall apart after a short period of time. Borates are often lumped together with water soluble evaporates such as halite and hanksite, which are commonly unstable. They were not easy to sell; so Jim became a master at trading them.

He once traded a beautiful big borax specimen to the curator of an Arizona museum for a beautiful Glove Mine wulfenite. She mistakenly thought that she could just call up Susie Davis (a wholesale dealer in Tucson) and buy another one. From time to time, he would find a museum whose curator would be willing to trade borates for other kinds of specimens. I did the same thing with zeolite specimens from India when I first brought them into the USA. They were new and exotic, and I was able to trade them for some wonderful specimens. Now most Indian zeolite specimens are a dime a dozen and many dealers won't handle them.

In my opinion Jim Minette was a successful collector for three reasons: First, he was knowledgeable and intelligent. Second, he worked hard at it for all of his adult life. Third, he had access through his job to a steady source of "free" specimens. But those specimens did not come easily; he had to work hard for them most of the time and spent thousands of hours collecting and preparing his finds.

THE COLLECTIONS

A postcard replica of a 1905 "Borax Is King" poster. Retired from hauling borax out of Death Valley, the Twenty Mule Team, along with a very feminine Borax Bill, Jr., began a career promoting borax products. The various forms of the Twenty Mule Team brand and logos have been in use since 1891.
Dawn Minette-Cooper collection
©U.S. Borax Inc.

THE BORATES
by James and Dawn Minette

Boron, the fifth element on the periodic table, is a hard brittle non-metal. It was first isolated in 1808 independently by Sir Humphry Davy (1778–1829) in London, and by a French team of Joseph Louis Gay-Lussac (1778–1850) and Louis Jacques Thénard (1777–1857) in Paris. The name boron was given to the element by Davy who combined the name **bor**ax (from which the element is derived) and carb**on** (which it resembled). Swedish chemist Jöns Jakob Berzelius (1779–1848) identified boron as an element in 1824, while General Electric chemist E. Weintraub is credited with being the first to produce pure boron. Weintraub accomplished this feat in the company's Lynn, Massachusetts lab in 1909.

Long before the element had been isolated or identified, jewelers were using boron compounds as fluxes for soldering gold. It was also used in cosmetics, creams, and cleaning compounds. Geoffrey Chaucer mentioned "boracic" (boric acid) in his description of the face of the Summoner (a lawyer for church courts), one of the pilgrims in his late fourteenth century *The Canterbury Tales*,

> *No quicksilver, lead ointment, tartar creams,*
> *No brimstone, no boracic, so it seems,*
> *Could make a salve that had the power to bite,*
> *Clean up or cure his whelks of knobby white*
> *Or purge the pimples sitting on his cheeks.*

"Boracic" was apparently used to treat acne in Medieval England. Most of the boron compounds used from the great Egyptian era thru the Greeks and the Romans were from Lake Yamdok Cho, south of Lhasa, Tibet. This locality supplied borax to the West through the eighteenth century.

Today, boron compounds are found in thousands of products including detergents, herbicides, pharmaceuticals, and fire retardants. They are also used in the manufacture of metal, glass, and enamel. Sodium borate is used as a water softening agent in some soap formulations. In addition, the element is vital to plants and is a common ingredient in fertilizers. Boron is a very effective absorber of neutrons and thus is helpful for preventing runaway chain reactions in nuclear reactors, a use for boron since the late-1940s. Boron is also an important component of some transistors, another recent use of this highly functional element.

Boron is the thirty-eighth most abundant element in the earth's crust, but because of its affinity to oxygen, native boron does not occur in nature; it is instead found in combination with other elements. Boron is an essential element of a host of other minerals including danburite, searlesite, dumortierite, and the tourmaline group minerals. However, the bulk of the Earth's boron is in the form of oxides and is sequestered in the class of minerals known as borates. Colemanite, ulexite, and borax are the most abundant boron ores.

Better than 100 borate class minerals have been identified to date, the most common of these and those best known among collectors are the hydrous borates, which have water incorporated into their structures. Anhydrous borates, which do not have water in their structures, are more stable than the hydrous borates but are relatively rare. Hydrous borates generally form as evaporate minerals in desert playas or dry lakes. Climate is critical to the preservation of some of the less stable hydrated borates, such as borax and kernite. Both of which alter with changes in the atmospheric water content and will fall apart in cabinets and drawers if not carefully preserved.

Boron

Editor's Note: A slightly modified version of the following section, written by James Minette, was published in *The Mineralogical Record* (1988), and was used with the permission from the publisher.

The Boron open pit and earlier U. S. Borax underground mines exploit the huge Kramer borate deposit in eastern Kern County, California. The main ore zone is an east-west trending sodium borate (borax and kernite) lens measuring roughly 1 by 3 kilometers with a maximum thickness of 100 meters.

The deposit was formed from hot springs about 18 million years ago in the middle of the Miocene (Barnard and Kistler, 1965; Whistler, 1965). Borax crystallized out in a playa lake, which had formed on the downward dropping side of an active fault. The lens is made up of layers of borax of varying richness, alternating with lakebed clays, and minor tuff beds. The borax is surrounded by a halo of green lakebed shales and a calcium borate facies, primarily ulexite.

Post-depositional faulting and folding of the orebody continued until about a million years ago and resulted in major distortion and a general dip to the south. The entire lakebed system was buried by typical arkosic desert alluvium. Today, the deepest ores lie some 350 meters below the surface, but there is indication that burial could have been as deep as 600 meters at one time.

The portions of the original orebody that were subjected to deepest burial underwent low-grade metamorphism to kernite through loss of water (Borax, $Na_2B_4O_5(OH)_4 \cdot 8H_2O \rightarrow$ Kernite, $Na_2B_4O_6(OH)_2 \cdot 3H_2O$). The result is that current mining is directed toward both minerals, the stratigraphically and structurally higher borax zone and the deeper kernite zone. The two ores must be processed separately.

Death Valley

The borate deposits in Death Valley, about 120 kilometers north-northeast of Boron, probably formed when sodium-borate-rich solutions came into contact with calcium-bearing material and mineralized as ulexite. Ground water reworked the ulexite, replacing the more soluble sodium with calcium to produce colemanite, present in the deposits around the valley. The main concentration of borates are on the east side of the valley and the largest concentration of them are around the mining camp of Ryan and Twenty Mule Team canyon. The occurrences are small orebodies in the lakebed sediments.

Our borate collection and collecting efforts focused primarily on specimens from the localities in these two districts.

"Clamshell" ULEXITE (Cat. No. B128), 21 cm wide, repaired
Hanging wall shale, West Baker Mine, Boron, Kern County, California
Collected by Jim Minette with Dawn Minette and John Seibel
Jeff Scovil photo

A group of three grayish "Mt. Fuji" shaped sprays of ulexite needle crystals with a dull to satiny luster. We collected these when we had access to the West Baker underground workings. The crystals formed in a shallow layer of brine and we recovered them from a mud seam on the back (top) of the stope, just above the mined-out borax bed. To collect the ulexite, one of us stood on a ladder and pried the mud seam loose while another person stood below and caught the falling detritus in a flat. As the material is brittle and fragile, it was difficult to get perfect, unbroken crystals. Most of the pieces had to be repaired after they were freed from the mud. The specimens were soaked in water and cleaned with dental tools in much the same way that fossils are prepared.

Left: Jim Minette collecting borax in the underground sumps of the West Baker Mine in January 1969. This area of the mine caved in about four months after this photo was taken. Walt Miller photo

Right: TINCALCONITE alteration pseudomorph after BORAX (Cat. No. B146), 15 cm wide
Underground sumps, Baker Mine, Boron, Kern County, California
Collected by Jim Minette; Jeff Scovil photo

A group of "Plaster of Paris" white tincalconite crystals that have altered from post-mining borax, which was found in one of the sumps that formed after the underground mines at Boron were abandoned. The crystals were pulled from the sumps as bright, clear borax, but after several years out of the mine, they altered to tincalconite. These elogated crystals are uncommon; blocky crystals are more typical from Boron; but various sumps produced distinctive crystals.

INDERITE and KURNAKOVITE (Cat. No. B002), crystal 7.3 cm long
Initial Pit, Boron Open Pit, Boron, Kern County, California
Purchased as part of the Vince Morgan Collection, 1992
Jeff Scovil photo

It is unusual to find kurnakovite in association with inderite. The two are paramorphs of one another and do not typically form together.

This is a superb group of open pocket kurnakovite crystals with terminated inderite crystals at one end of the specimen. It is the finest combination piece known. It was sprayed to prevent a film from forming on the surfaces of the crystals.

TUNELLITE on ULEXITE (Cat. No. B067), 12 cm tall
Extension 5, Boron Open Pit, Boron, Kern County, California
Purchased as part of the Vince Morgan Collection, 1992
Jeff Scovil photo

Richard Erd, Vincent Morgan and J.R. Clark identified and described the strontium borate tunellite ($SrB_6O_9(OH)_2 \cdot 3H_2O$) in 1961. Dawn's (now deceased) second husband Danny Cooper found the type material some four years earlier in the mine in Boron. The new species was named in honor of Dr. George Gerard Tunell, Jr. (1900–1996), a geology professor at UCLA. The type material is at the Smithsonian Institution.

Equant crystals reaching widths of 5 centimeters with a pearly luster were found loose or in association with hydroboracite and in some cases with "cottonball" ulexite. Some of the crystals are translucent, while others are included with mud. The species has since been found in several Death Valley localities and in some of the extensive Turkish borate deposits.

This tunellite on realgar-stained ulexite is possibly the finest known matrix specimen of the mineral. It is one of a number of large tunellite crystals found on the dumps at Boron in the mid-1960s. The exact origin of the specimens is not clear, but they are known to have been found in the overburden of the orebody.

COLEMANITE on CALCITE (Cat. No. B127), 19 cm wide
Extension 17, Boron Open Pit, Boron, Kern County, California
Collected by Jim Minette in 1978
Jeff Scovil photo

Colemanite ($CaB_3O_4(OH)_3 \cdot H_2O$) and calcite ($CaCO_3$) are found above the orebody in many places in the mine, particularly those that were cut by faults. Colemanite and calcite are, in most cases, secondary minerals resulting from the dissolution of ulexite ($NaCaB_5O_6(OH)_6 \cdot 5H_2O$) when it comes in contact with ground water. Much of the colemanite in Boron is massive, but sharp crystals do form in vugs within the massive material.

Jim collected a lot of colemanite throughout his years in Boron, including this large spray on botryoidal calcite. Under long wave ultraviolet light, the calcite fluoresces bright yellow, and the colemanite bright blue-white. The colemanite is also strongly phosphorescent.

COLEMANITE on CALCITE (Cat. No. B131), 17 cm wide
Initial Pit, Boron Open Pit, Boron, Kern County, California
Collected by Howard Pomtier, a foreman at the mine during the early years of the open pit, and acquired from him around 1960
Jeff Scovil photo

This specimen of lustrous botryoidal calcite with large, sharp, colemanite crystals to 3 centimeters was recovered from the mine prior to our moving to Boron.

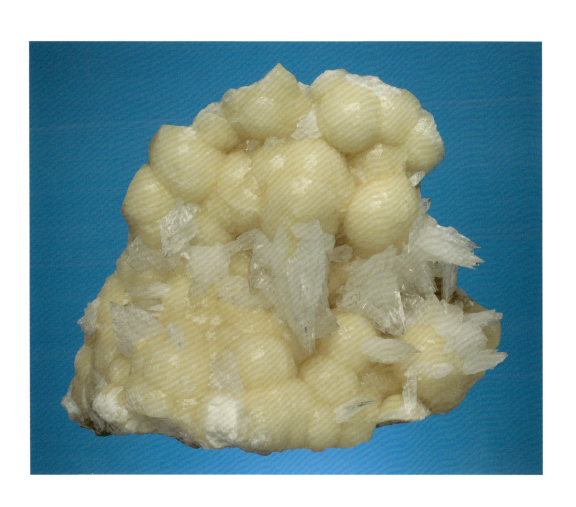

ORPIMENT on COLEMANITE with minor ORPIMENT in CALCITE (Cat. No. B135), 12 cm wide
Extension 3, Boron Open Pit, Boron, Kern County, California
Collected by Jim Minette in May, 1961
Jeff Scovil photo

COLEMANITE and CALCITE replacing ULEXITE (Cat. No. B164), 10 cm tall
Extension 16, Boron Open Pit, Boron, Kern County, California
Collected by Jim Minette
Jeff Scovil photo

This specimen of parallel, acicular ulexite crystals with straw-colored calcite after ulexite pseudomorphs and colemanite is a good example of the replacement series from the sodium-calcium borate (ulexite) to calcium borate (colemanite). It is a fine combination of three of the most common minerals at Boron.

COLEMANITE on CALCITE (Cat. No. B181), 9 cm tall
Extension 18, Boron Open Pit, Boron, Kern County, California
Collected by Jim Minette
Jeff Scovil photo

Single colemanite crystals are rare from Boron. Jim recovered this one from an unconsolidated ulexite seam located in extension 18 of the pit. He enjoyed collecting this specimen because it was easy digging.

ULEXITE on CALCITE (Cat. No. B107), 20 cm wide
Boron Open Pit, Boron, Kern County, California
Purchased in 1992
Part of the Vince Morgan collection; Jeff Scovil photo

COLEMANITE included with PARAREALGAR (Cat. No. T1109), 2.4 cm tall
Extension 2, Boron Open Pit, Boron, Kern County, California
Purchased with the Vince Morgan thumbnails on May 5, 1992
Jeff Scovil photo

This ball of blocky colemanite crystals is colored a uniform yellow by pararealgar. It sits on a stem of yellow colemanite and represents an unusual habit for Boron.

PROBERTITE (Cat. No. B142), 9.8 cm tall
Footwall Shale, Extension 18, Boron Open Pit, Boron, Kern County, California
Collected by Jim and Dawn Minette, 1987
Jeff Scovil photo

The old Baker Mine at Boron is the type locality for probertite ($NaCaB_5O_7(OH)_4 \cdot 3H_2O$). This specimen was featured in an article in *The Mineralogical Record* (1988) that Jim wrote about the find,

> A significant find of clusters of long radial crystals of probertite in shale was made in March, 1987, at the Boron, California, open pit mine of the U.S. Borax Company. The find, in the footwall calcium borate zone, has provided the most aesthetic specimens of the mineral ever found... Several boxes of probertite-bearing shale were collected for cleaning, yielding about 20 flats of specimens showing several growth habits... Preparation and preservation of the specimens was crucial in this dig; they were almost unrecognizable as good specimens when found. Considerable experimentation was done before the best technique for shale removal was found... Short soaking in water, from 15 minutes to an hour, followed by repeated cycles of rinsing and dental tool picking proved the best. After several cycles, noticeable weakening of the specimen becomes evident... When the weakness point was observed, the specimens were dried and lightly sprayed with clear acrylic or similar clear spray paint. This spray gave just enough bonding to the already cleaned areas that the last deep crevice cleaning could be done safely. Several great cabinet specimens became nice miniatures before this lesson was learned.

Left: The Corkscrew Mine, circa 1978; Jim Minette photo

Right: COLEMANITE after INYOITE (Cat. No. B126), 16 cm wide
Corkscrew Mine, Corkscrew Canyon, Furnace Creek Wash, Inyo County, Death Valley, California
Collected by Jim Minette
Jeff Scovil photo

The mine was a pod of ore, which was originally inyoite but was replaced by meyerhofferite and eventually colemanite. Crystals throughout the mine showed relict structures of the previous minerals. In this specimen, colemanite formed over inyoite crystals. The Furnace Creek Wash area is the type locality for colemanite.

This specimen is a product of one of the collecting trips we made to the Corkscrew Mine over many years. It was one of our favorite collecting spots. Each of our sons remembers being conscripted by their father to help collect in the mine. There were large, deep vugs in the pillars that often contained "floater" specimens of colemanite. Some of these holes weren't large enough for an adult to fit into, but a small boy could be urged into them. All of our boys were glad when they became too large to be "stuffed" into the pockets.

HYDROBORACITE (Cat. No. B176), 5 cm wide
Thompson Mine, Ryan, Furnace Creek Wash, Death Valley, Inyo County, California
Collected by Jim Minette and Dave Wilber on January 1, 1972
Jeff Scovil photo

This specimen of radial hydroboracite sprays was found on a collecting trip with Dave Wilber and represented a new find for the Death Valley area. Jim and Dave wrote an article on the occurrence for *The Mineralogical Record* (1973). What follows is an excerpt from that article:

> The Thompson Mine is located about two miles west of Ryan in Furnace Creek Wash, Death Valley, California. The mine was developed and worked in the mid-1920s. It was shut down in the 1930s, and worked briefly again in the 1960s by the Kern County Land Company ... The deposit is primarily colemanite, which occurs as beds with lake bed shales of the Furnace Creek formation in a long, tightly-folded, synclinal structure. The mine is opened by three vertical shafts which reach a maximum depth of 120 feet. Three levels take off from the shafts, and several small stopes are found between the levels. These workings produced several thousand tons of colemanite during two production periods ...

> ... The hydroboracite described herein was found by the authors on the bottom level of the mine in vugs with small colemanite crystals. At first glance in the mine, it looks much like colemanite. The first material collected was literally hanging out of a wall—a rarity today.

Over two days of collecting Jim, Dave, and two other unspecified collectors recovered three or four flats of top grade specimens and another ten flats of "good, well-crystallized representative material." The largest specimen they collected (20 cm tall) went to the Smithsonian Institution.

> In case people tend to forget the effort involved in field collecting, eight hours in a two day period were spent on [the Smithsonian] piece, mostly with a four-pound sledge hammer while working overhead from an impromptu scaffold!

CELESTINE on COLEMANITE (Cat. No. SC008), 14 cm wide
Boraxo Pit #3, Thompson Mine, Ryan, Furnace Creek Wash, Death Valley, Inyo County, California
Collected by Jim Minette, David Minette, and Curtis Petrey
Jesse La Plante photo

Jim Minette, Gehard Mühle, Paul Hartman and mine superintendent Chuck Longshore collected the bulk of this unique find over a few months in 1972. As Jim and Gehard Mühle (1974) described it,

> The pit encountered a heavy water inflow in the bottom at about 140 feet in depth... The water brought a marked change in the nature of the orebody. Above the water table the clay was dry, hard, light tan-colored, and relatively iron-free. Below the water table, the clay was soft, sticky, almost black colored, with probable microscopic dispersions of iron sulfides (unidentified). An oxide-sulfide zone relationship in a borate deposit is a bit novel, but there it was. The old guideline, "look at the matrix color to tell Boron and Death Valley colemanite apart," no longer held true...

> In mid-summer, Tenneco finished mining the upper layers of the ore and broke into the thin layers of coarsely crystalline colemanite in the very bottom of the eastern end of Pit No. 1 at about 150 feet of depth... The collecting zone was about six feet thick by 150 feet long, dipping at 70 to 90 degrees into the pit bottom. Within the six-foot zone, two very prominent beds about two feet apart and each only a foot or two thick produced by far the bulk of the specimens. The largest crystals tended to be in the lower bed, although both seams produced superb material...

> A painful (now laughable) facet of collecting at the Thompson were the cuts received from sharp cleavages. There was, of necessity, a lot of hand removal of debris that fell into the deep pockets. Much of this was in the form of razor-sharp colemanite cleavages. Once, after one of the authors had received a particularly nasty cut, and the area had taken on a vivid red color, the Mine Superintendent commented on the beautiful "Type-O" colemanite. The name stuck, and many a jibe about "O" colemanite was made later when anyone cut himself. Gloves were a necessity.

COLEMANITE (Cat. No. B203), 27 cm wide
Boraxo Pit #3, Thompson Mine, Ryan, Furnace Creek Wash, Death Valley, Inyo County, California
Collected by Jim Minette, 1972
Jeff Scovil photo

Jim and Gehard Mühle (1974) on collecting the great Thompson Mine colemanite find of 1972:

> Initial collecting problems were caused by the mining method. A Caterpillar D-9 ripper-dozer was used to tear out the ore. As the area was below the water table in an area of high clay content, an inspection of the pit floor showed a hopelessly jumbled muddy mess ...
>
> The upper section of the pocket area passed into the east wall, and here much of the collecting time was spent. The pockets were well exposed, clean and dry—and too hard for really good collecting. Some nice "floaters" came out, but it was a beautiful siren tempting the collector to spend hours of work for a few choice pieces.
>
> The real breakthrough came when the D-9 dozed away loose muck from the pit floor and exposed the tops of some fresh pockets. Anything loose was readily removed, but the solid walls, where the largest crystals grew, were usually too hard to work. A chisel merely caused the coarse crystals to fall apart between their intergrown faces. The management again came to the rescue. They had to rip the area for mining anyway, so the Mine Superintendent had the dozer carefully rip the pocket area—at least as carefully as you can expect from a 50-ton D-9. This was ideal because it cracked the area between the ripper teeth enough to allow proper collecting, yet it did not interfere with mining operations.

COLEMANITE (Cat. No. B153), 13 cm wide
White Monster Mine, Ryan, Furnace Creek Wash, Death Valley, Inyo County, California
Collected by Jim Minette; Jeff Scovil photo

Death Valley, circa 1978; Jim Minette photo

MEYERHOFFERITE (Cat. No. B185), 4 cm wide
Mt. Blanco, Twenty Mule Team Wash, Furnace Creek District, Inyo County, California
Collected by Jim Minette
Jeff Scovil photo

Mt. Blanco was one of the small orebodies in Death Valley that belonged to U.S. Borax. When Jim was the Mine Manager at Boron, responsibility for the U.S. Borax properties in Death Valley also fell to him. He was thus able to collect minerals in the mines more or less freely.

Mt. Blanco is the type locality for both meyerhofferite ($Ca_2B_6O_6(OH)_{10} \cdot 2H_2O$) and inyoite ($CaB_3O_3(OH)_5 \cdot 4H_2O$). The former was named for German chemist Wilhelm Meyerhoffer (1864–1906), who was the first to synthesize the material in the lab. Inyoite was named for Inyo County. The type material for meyerhofferite is at Harvard University in Cambridge, Massachusetts.

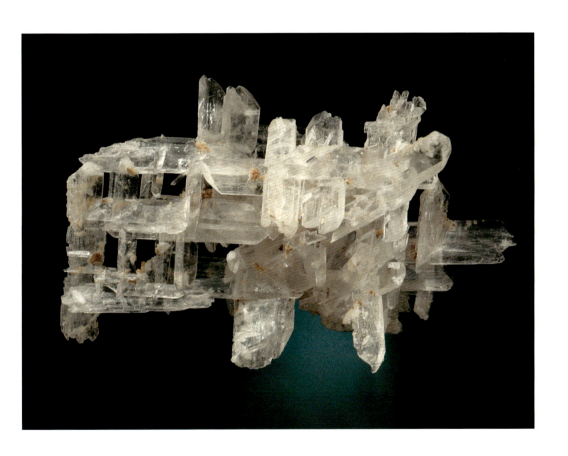

Right: CELESTINE on COLEMANITE (Cat. No. WW112), 12 cm tall
Level 1490, Billie Mine, Ryan District, Furnace Creek Wash, Death Valley, California
Purchased in 1994 from an ex Billie Mine employee
Jeff Scovil photo

The largest celestine crystals known at the time from Death Valley make up this cabinet specimen, which we bought in 1994 as part of a collection of minerals from the Billie Mine.

Below: A January 10, 2010 photo of the Billie Mine head frame and support buildings. The site is closed and is showing signs of neglect; Bob Griffis photo

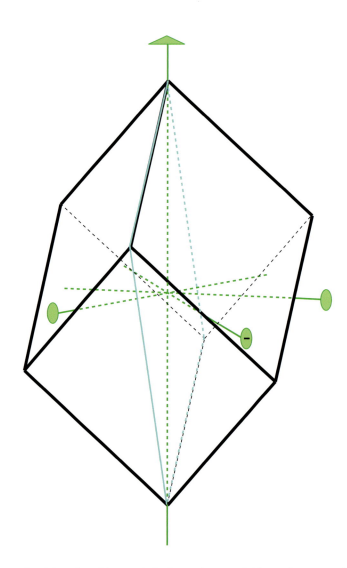

Symmetry elements of smithsonite. The ovals indicate the two-fold rotation axes, the triangle indicates the three-fold axis, and the blue lines indicate the position of one of the mirror planes that are perpendicular to each two-fold axis. R. Peter Richards graphic

THE SMITHSONITES
a summary of form by R. Peter Richards

Smithsonite is a carbonate of zinc, $ZnCO_3$ and belongs to the rhombohedral carbonates, all of which have the same crystal structure, differing only in the cation that is present. Along with smithsonite (zinc), this group includes calcite (calcium), siderite (iron), rhodochrosite (manganese), magnesite (magnesium), sphaerocobaltite (cobalt), otavite (cadmium), and gaspéite (nickel). Smithsonite occurs in far fewer habits than does the more familiar calcite. One indication of this is that Goldschmidt's *Atlas of Crystal Forms* has 13 drawings of smithsonite crystals but 153 *pages* of drawings of calcite crystals!

Smithsonite is found primarily in oxidized zones of zinc-bearing ore deposits (the slag deposits at Laurium, Greece being a special human-influenced example). In these deposits, smithsonite forms by alteration of primary zinc minerals, especially sphalerite. This alteration releases zinc into solution, primarily into groundwater seeping down from the surface, where it interacts with carbon dioxide dissolved in the water, precipitating smithsonite.

Rhombohedral carbonates crystallize in the scalenohedral class of the rhombohedral division of the hexagonal symmetry system, with symmetry $\bar{3}\ 2/m$. This shorthand symbol indicates that smithsonite has one axis of three-fold symmetry (c-axis) with an inversion center and three axes of two-fold symmetry (a-axes), all of which are in a plane perpendicular to the three-fold axis and are 120 degrees apart from one another. Each two-fold axis has a mirror plane of symmetry perpendicular to it. The three-fold axis relates each face to the two faces 120 degrees apart around the c-axis. The inversion center relates each face to another face diagonally opposite through the center of the crystal. Each two-fold axis relates each face to the face opposite it by a rotation of 180 degrees around the axis, and each mirror plane relates each face to another face opposite it, as if reflected in a mirror. This combination of symmetry elements leads to forms that tend to have either six (rhombohedra and prisms) or twelve (scalenohedra, bipyramids, and diprisms) faces, although the pinacoid consists of just two faces, at opposite ends of the crystal and perpendicular to the c-axis.

The crystal structure of the rhombohedral carbonates is simple, with layers of cations alternating along the c-axis with layers of carbonate groups, which are triangular arrays of three oxygens with a carbon in the center. Because the cations of the different species have different sizes, the unit cell (the basic building block of the crystal structure) also differs in size, primarily along the c-axis. Compared to calcite, smithsonite has a smaller unit cell, is denser, harder, and has a higher luster, the latter a consequence of higher refractive indices.

In spite of its few habits, there is enormous variety of colors, associations, localities, and forms of smithsonite. Mineral dealer Rob Lavinsky said of The Minette Collection, "Its strength is in its focus and the depth of the suites." The strength to which Rob refers is certainly expressed in the smithsonites, which reflect a variety that can only be amassed over a lifetime of collecting.

SMITHSONITE and GOETHITE (Cat. No. S010), 18 cm tall
Kelly Mine, Magdalena district, Socorro County, New Mexico
Obtained in a trade with the New Mexico School of Mines Museum in 1964
Jeff Scovil photo

This specimen was in the basement of the New Mexico School of Mines Museum (now the New Mexico Bureau of Geology and Mineral Resources Museum) when we visited in the mid-1960s. Then-director, Alvin "Lefty" Thompson, was willing to trade specimens from the non-display collection. This was an old time piece whose mate is and was on display at the museum.

Above: The renowned Kelly Mine, circa 2007; Kevin Dixon photo

Left: SMITHSONITE after CERUSSITE (Cat. No. S035), 6 cm tall
Kelly Mine, Magdalena district, Socorro County, New Mexico
Obtained in a trade with the New Mexico School of Mines Museum in 1965
New Mexico Bureau of Geology and Mineral Resources specimen (No. 16785); Jeff Scovil photo

SMITHSONITE (Cat. No. S040), 11 cm tall
Kelly Mine, Magdalena district, Socorro County, New Mexico
Obtained in a trade with The New Mexico School of Mines Museum in 1965
It was repatriated in 2008, after the collection was sold.
New Mexico Bureau of Geology and Mineral Resources specimen (No. 17457)
Jeff Scovil photo

When we bought this specimen, we were toilet-training our boys, and Jim noted, "If we found something like this in the middle of the floor, we'd spank one of the kids."

SMITHSONITE (Cat. No. S251), 13 cm wide, repaired
400 Level, Kelly Mine, Magdalena district, Socorro County, New Mexico
Purchased in 1990 (ex Tom McKee)
Dan Adams collection; Jeff Scovil photo

This from Pete Richards,

> In contrast to calcite, which frequently occurs as sharp single crystals and displays many crystal habits, well-formed crystals of smithsonite are relatively rare. Smithsonite most often occurs as undulating surfaces coating the matrix: the terms "botryoidal" (like a cluster of grapes) or "reniform" (kidney-like) are often used to describe such specimens. Stalactitic smithsonite is also fairly common. In all of these types of specimens, the smithsonite is composed of hundreds to millions of individual crystals, whose crystal form is largely to completely obscured by the mass that they form together. The shape of this mass is mostly a reflection of the surface on which it grows, and of the "competition" of individual crystals to keep from being covered up by their neighbors and thereby ceasing to grow.

SMITHSONITE (Cat. No. S241), 9 cm wide
400 Level, Kelly Mine, Magdalena district, Socorro County, New Mexico
Purchased from Tony Otero in October, 1992
Steve Neely collection; Jeff Scovil photo

This was part of a large lot of smithsonite specimens we bought from Tony Otero in 1992. I (DM) remember sitting in Tony's cellar on a painted Mexican children's chair while Jim and Tony dickered over price.

SMITHSONITE (Cat. No. S400)
30 cm wide
Kelly Mine, Magdalena district
Socorro County, New Mexico
Jeff Scovil photo

SMITHSONITE on CERUSSITE (Cat. No. S002), 10 cm wide
Tsumeb Mine, Otjikoto Region, Namibia
Purchased from John Watson in 1964
Jeff Scovil photo

SMITHSONITE (Cat. No. S013), 7 cm wide
Tsumeb Mine, Otjikoto Region, Namibia
Purchased from Crystal Gallery in 1964
Marty Zinn collection; Jeff Scovil photo

This was our first big smithsonite purchase, and we thought long and hard before we bought it. The price? $90! Smithsonite was becoming a passion. The variety of color, habit, luster, and associations found in the smithsonite from Tsumeb alone makes it a nice collectible, while fine specimens are just rare enough to keep the hunt interesting.

SMITHSONITE (Cat. No. S135)
18 cm wide
9th Level, Tsumeb Mine
Otjikoto Region, Namibia
Purchased from Minerals Unlimited in 1972
Marty Zinn collection; Jesse La Plante photo

Norm Dawson had sold this cabinet-size specimen to Paul Zimmerman in 1960.

SMITHSONITE (Cat. No. S160), 11.3 cm wide
39th Level, Tsumeb Mine, Otjikoto Region, Namibia
Purchased from Rock Currier in 1977
Upper photo by Jeff Scovil
Detail (left) by Jesse La Plante

SMITHSONITE with ROSASITE (Cat. No. S199), 6.5 cm wide
Tsumeb Mine, Otjikoto Region, Namibia
Purchased from Prosper Williams in 1979
John Smolski photo

This from crystallographer Pete Richards

> When smithsonite does occur as well-formed single crystals, they are usually of simple rhombohedral habit (above). Scalenohedra (facing page), if present, are usually minor forms modifying the edges or corners of the rhombohedron. Crystal faces are often rounded, as in the "grains of wheat" habit from the Kelly Mine in Magdalena, Socorro County, New Mexico, or may be "hoppered" to varying degrees. Other faces belonging to different forms on the same crystals are flat, as is the cleavage, indicating that the crystal structure itself is not distorted, but that the conditions of growth have not favored the development of flat faces for all of the forms on the crystal.

Above: SMITHSONITE (Cat. No. S031), 5.5 cm tall
Tsumeb Mine, Otjikoto Region, Namibia
Acquired through trade with Merle R. Reid of Crystal Gallery in 1967
Jesse La Plante photo

Right: SMITHSONITE on GOETHITE (Cat. No. S217), 7.5 cm tall
Tsumeb Mine, Otjikoto Region, Namibia
Purchased from Ken Roberts at the California Federation Show in San Jose, 1984
Marty Zinn collection; Jeff Scovil photo

SMITHSONITE on TENNANTITE (Cat. No. S230), 16 cm wide
Tsumeb Mine, Otjikoto Region, Namibia
Purchased from Miriam and Julius Zweibel in 1987
Jeff Scovil photo

A fine specimen of tennantite with a thin coating of clear-to-pale-pink smithsonite.

SMITHSONITE (Cat. No. S258), 10 cm tall
Upper Levels, Tsumeb Mine, Otjikoto Region, Namibia
Purchased as part of the Vince Morgan collection
Steve Neely collection; Jeff Scovil photo

Clifford Frondel gave Vince Morgan this superb specimen from the Harvard University collection in thanks for Vince's working with him on identifying gerstleyite, $Na_2(Sb,As)_8S_{13} \cdot 2(H_2O)$, a mineral for which the Baker Mine at Boron, Kern County, California is the type locality. The mineral is named for James Mack Gerstley (1907-2007), former president of the Pacific Coast Borax Company.

SMITHSONITE (Cat. No. S327), 9 cm tall
Tsumeb Mine, Otjikoto Region, Namibia
Purchased from C. Carter Rich on September 17, 2004
Marty Zinn collection; Jeff Scovil photo;

Dawn bought this specimen after Jim died. She purchased it from Carter Rich at the Denver Show. It had been in Ed David's collection.

SMITHSONITE (Cat. No. S328), 9 cm wide
Tsumeb Mine, Otjikoto Region, Namibia
Purchased from Doug Wallace (Mineral Search) on November 13, 2004
Dan and Diana Weinrich collection; Jeff Scovil photo

Clive Queit collected this specimen on August 15, 1986. This specimen was also purchased by Dawn after Jim died.

Above: SMITHSONITE (Cat. No. S126), 7 cm wide
Berg Aukas Mine, Grootfontein, Namibia
Purchased form Walt Lidstrom, 1970
Bill and Diana Dameron collection; Jesse Fisher photo

Right: SMITHSONITE stalagmite (Cat. No. S170), 20 cm tall
8th Level, Berg Aukas Mine, Grootfontein, Namibia
Purchased from Brad van Scriver in February, 1978
Jeff Scovil photo

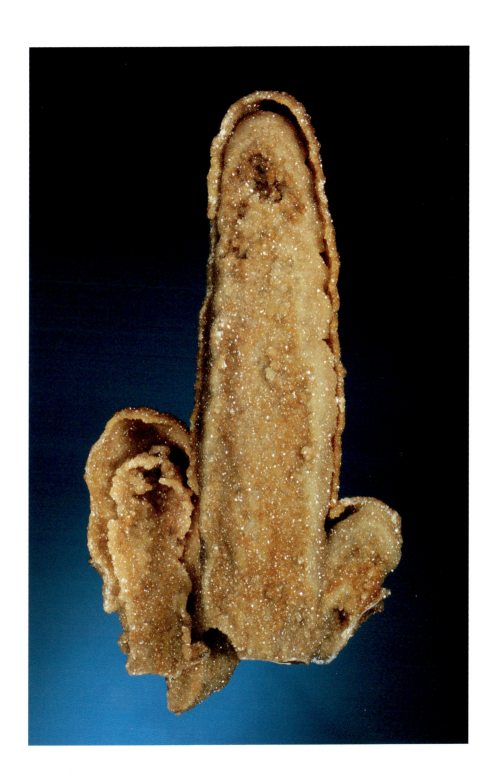

SMITHSONITE (Cat. No. S229), 14 cm wide
Berg Aukas Mine, Grootfontein district, Otjozondjupa region, Namibia
Purchased from Kristalle in February 1987 (ex E. Mitchell Gunnell collection)
John Maxwell collection; Jeff Scovil photo

SMITHSONITE on WILLEMITE
(Cat. No. S222), 20 cm wide
Berg Aukas Mine, Grootfontein district,
Otjozondjupa region, Namibia
Purchased from J. Conetts in 1986
Jeff Scovil photo

The back side of this light green smithsonite specimen is covered with botryoidal, dark olive-green willemite. There is also some micro black descloizite on the piece.

SMITHSONITE with PARAHOPEITE (Cat. No. S286), 8 cm wide
Broken Hill Mine, Kabwe, Zambia
Obtained through an exchange with C. Carter Rich in May, 2001
Jeff Scovil photo

Using scanning electron microscope, Gary Zito at the Colorado School of Mines confirmed that the white ball is indeed a zinc phosphate, but additional analysis is required to determine precisely which one. The specimen was previously owned by Phil Scalisi.

WILLEMITE pseudomorph after SMITHSONITE (Cat. No. S282), 9 cm wide
Berg Aukas Mine, Grootfontein district, Otjozondjupa region, Namibia
Purchased from Wayne Thompson and Gary Hansen in February, 2000
Marty Zinn collection; Jeff Scovil photo

Jim said that this pseudomorph was the best of its type that he had ever seen.

SMITHSONITE (Cat. No. S240), 18.5 cm wide
Union Mine, 400 Level, Cerro Gordo, Inyo County, California
Purchased from Bill Larson in 1994 (ex Josie Scripps)
Jeff Scovil photo

This botryoidal blue green plate was from the Josie Scripps collection, which she had gifted to Bill Larson. Years later, we bought the specimen from him. Josie had been given it by a friend who found it under the tramway where an ore bucket had dropped. Jim later found the spot and collected a lesser quality piece or two.

SMITHSONITE (Cat. No. S134), 13 cm wide
Mina Massua, Sardinia, Italy
Purchased from Rock Currier in February, 1973 (ex Cruden collection)
Jeff Scovil photo

SMITHSONITE (Cat. No. S300), 11 cm tall
Morning Star Mine, Rush, Marion County, Arkansas
Jeff Scovil photo

Pete Richards:

    Between specimens for which the form is determined by multi-crystalline masses and those determined by single crystals are interesting specimens in which there is some ambiguity about whether the individual units are single crystals or not. A good example of this interesting middle ground is provided by the specimen pictured on the facing page. It is composed of discrete crystals that have the saddle-shaped form typically associated with dolomite.

    Another example is provided by the "bowtie" smithsonite habit from Rush, Arkansas. In these beautiful yellow microcrystals, each end is like a club with three-fold cross section, with the edges of one end corresponding to the middles of the surfaces of the other end. The bowties are composed of rounded undulatory surfaces, but the aggregate shape is consistent with the symmetry of smithsonite.

    In these crystals, the crystal structure is distorted in a systematic way, leading to the formation of multiple crystals, each of which is nearly but not exactly parallel to its neighbors. Each distortion is in the same direction, leading to the formation of a macroscopically curved surface composed of many flat or nearly flat faces belonging to many tiny sub-parallel crystals. How does one decide whether to call these specimens "special multi-crystal aggregates" or "distorted single crystals." Perhaps the distinction is not important, but these examples of smithsonite form an interesting bridge between specimens dominated by discrete single crystals and specimens dominated by botryoidal or stalactitic surfaces composed of myriads of unrecognizable tiny crystals.

SMITHSONITE (Cat. No. S137), 14 cm wide
Morning Star Mine, Rush, Marion County, Arkansas
Trade from the Smithsonian Institution in January, 1975
George Witters collection; Jeff Scovil photo

This specimen was tan-colored when Jim got it, but he treated it with acid to take off the top layer of smithsonite and reveal the beautiful "turkey fat" layer he saw in the specimen.

SMITHSONITE (Cat. No. S215), 13 cm wide
Touissit, Oujda, Morocco
Purchased from Victor Yount in January 1984
Steve Neely collection; Jeff Scovil photo

We purchased this from Victor at one of the famed pre-Tucson parties at Wayne and Dona Leicht's. The parties were always great, and a bit of mineral trading was a side benefit. This specimen has a velvety luster, which cannot be captured by even the most accomplished photographer.

SMITHSONITE on CORONADITE (Cat. No. S083), 13 cm wide
Broken Hill, New South Wales, Australia
Dan Adams collection; Jesse La Plante photo

SMITHSONITE (Cat. No. S267), 6.5 cm wide
Touissit Mine, Oujda, Morocco
Purchased from Cal Graeber in May 1995
Marty Zinn collection; Jeff Scovil photo

SMITHSONITE (Cat. No. S281), 7 cm wide
Broken Hill Mine, Kabwe, Zambia
Purchased from the Gary Hansen collection via Wayne Thompson in February 2000
Jeff Scovil photo

PHOSPHOPHYLLITE (Cat. No. T0241), 2 cm tall
Cerro Rico, Potosí City, Potosí Department, Bolivia
Trade/Purchase with Peter Bancroft in 1968
Gail and Jim Spann collection; Jeff Scovil photo

Pete Bancroft bought this thumbnail, along with a group of other specimens, from a dying miner in late-1967 while Peter was on a trip to Bolivia. The phosphophyllite pocket occurred in massive marcasite at a depth of about 2000 feet.

RHODONITE (Cat. No. T0312), 2.5 cm tall
1700 Level, Zinc Corp. Mine, Broken Hill
New South Wales, Australia
Purchased from Peter Bancroft in 1971
Rich Olsen collection; Jeff Scovil photo

According to Albert Chapman, who bought this specimen from a miner, it is one of the four best crystals to have come out of the mine. A foreman saw a small pocket in the face prior to blasting and saved the specimens.

THE THUMBNAILS
by Gloria A. Staebler

In 1999 toward the end of my mineral dealing career, *The Mineralogical Record* publisher Wendell Wilson came into my room in Tucson and purchased a baseball-size chunk of matrix with a small, gemmy, londonite crystal buried in it. The mineral was newly described and the specimens were pricey; so when he told me that he was going to trim the rock and make a thumbnail out of it, I was a little shocked by what I perceived as his recklessness. The next day, he came back into my room with a beautiful little specimen consisting of a nearly complete glassy yellow crystal with just enough matrix to nicely enhance the gem. I didn't recognize the specimen until he told me that it was the one that he had bought from me the day before. In that moment, I caught a glimpse of the particular vision, knowledge, and nerve required of the thumbnail collector.

Rock Currier got Jim and Dawn's thumbnail collection started around 1964 by giving Dawn a couple of specimens. At first the collection was hers, but then Jim began to take an interest in the "little specimens," and it became *their* collection. By 1965 they were competing with their thumbnails. And at the 1966 Las Vegas show, they took the American Federation of Mineral Societies' national trophy for thumbnails. In short order they had catapulted themselves to the center of the thumbnail collecting scene. So familiar were they among thumbnail collectors, that in 1967, when Gerry Blair found a nice thumbnail, he gloated in his One by One column in *Gems & Minerals*, "Eat your heart out, Jim Minette."

Jim and Dawn searched, trimmed, bought, traded, and sold thumbnails. They debated the rules for competition, joined organizations, tried, won, and failed. In 1984, at San Diego, they took the AFMS thumbnail trophy for a second time, also winning the trophy for the best mineral display in the show. That was their warm-up for Tucson, where they were planning to compete for the prestigious McDole Trophy (since renamed the Desautels Award). At the 1985 Tucson Gem and Mineral Society show, they won the McDole with their thumbnails. Later, fellow thumbnail collector Allan Young said he had been in awe of and had studied their winning case. In his mind, Jim and Dawn had "redefined thumbnail collecting with those specimens, each a miniature sculpture, carefully selected, trimmed, and displayed."

After winning the McDole, the Minettes stopped competing with their thumbnails and relaxed the one-by-one inch rule for their own collection. When Dawn displayed the collection in Springfield, Massachusetts, she mentioned that it was a collection of small minerals, not specifically thumbnail specimens, noting, "If you are not competing for trophies, there are too many fine specimens that shouldn't be passed over because of slight size constraints."

Certainly gram for gram, and probably specimen for specimen, the thumbnails were the most valuable part of the Minette Collection. While the "little specimens" may not represent their most back-breaking work, it is a manifestation of their courage as well as of their pioneering vision.

NEPTUNITE (Cat. No. T0371), 2.5 cm wide
Dallas Gem Mine, San Benito County, California
Acquired through a trade with Bill Larson in November, 1971
Alex Schauss collection; Jeff Scovil photo

PYROXMANGITE (Cat. No. T0618), 2 cm wide
14 Level, South Mine, Broken Hill, New South Wales, Australia
Traded with Demetrius Pohl in December 1975
Alex Schauss collection; Jeff Scovil photo

We bought this thumbnail as "rhodonite" but Howard K. Worner, author of *Minerals of Broken Hill*, examined the specimen and told us that it was pyroxmangite. This specimen was part of our McDole Trophy-winning case.

Above: WOODHOUSEITE
(Cat. No. T0308), 3 cm wide
Champion (White Mountain) Mine, White
Mountains, Mono County, California
Al Ordway recovered this specimen in July 1970,
while collecting with Jim and David Minette
Alex Schauss collection; Jeff Scovil photo

Jim trimmed this specimen down to a thumbnail, and it was included in our McDole Trophy winning case. Al found a second good crystal on the same trip, but he kept it as part of a cabinet-size specimen.

Right: SCORODITE (Cat. No, T0721), 2.5 cm tall
Tsumeb Mine, Otjikoto Region, Namibia
Purchased from Zweibel's in August 1977
Wendell Wilson collection; Jeff Scovil photo

Right: SMITHSONITE on AURICHALCITE
(Cat. No. T0659), 3 cm tall
Kelly Mine, Magdalena district, Socorro County, New Mexico
Traded from David Eidahl in January 1977
Wayne Thompson specimen; Jeff Scovil photo

Jim liked this stalactite because it was a bit suggestive; I liked it because it was a good color thumbnail. Wayne Thompson sold the specimen to David Eidahl, and it was pictured in *Rock and Gem* (vol. 2). After I sold the collection, Wayne Thompson bought it back.

Left: HESSITE with minor GOLD
(Cat. No. T0795), 2.5 cm tall
Botés, Alba County, Romania
Purchased from Pala Properties in October 1979
Jeff Scovil photo

PARAMELACONITE (Cat. No. T0755), 2 cm tall
Copper Queen Mine, Bisbee, Cochise County, Arizona
Purchased from Rock Currier in May 1978
Evan Jones collection; Jesse La Plante photo

This group with minor malachite and connellite is one of four known paramelaconite specimens from Bisbee and is the only one in private hands. It was the rarest mineral in our collection. Rock Currier got it through a trade with Bryn Mawr College; it had been part of the Vaux collection.

Jim wanted this specimen in the worst way, and he offered Rock $3500 for it—a huge sum in the mid-1970s. Rock refused and kept the specimen, holding on to it until he had a girlfriend whom he wanted to impress. At that point, he offered to sell us the specimen if we would buy a stereo system for his house and pay him the balance in cash. Jim jumped at the offer and Rock got his sound system. The funny thing was that when the young woman went to visit Rock: he turned up the stereo to show her what it would do, and she told him that it gave her a headache and asked him to turn it down.

When this specimen sold in Tucson, 2008, it commanded what was thought to be the highest price ever paid for a thumbnail.

Upper: VESZELYITE (Cat. No. T0874), 2.6 cm tall
Max and Jon Sigerman collection; Jeff Scovil photo

Lower: VESZELYITE (Cat. No. WW325), 5 cm tall, repaired
Dan and Diana Weinrich collection; Jeff Scovil photo

Black Pine Mine, Flint Creek Valley, John Long Mountains, Philipsburg, Granite County, Montana
Purchased in December 1981

The first time we heard of veszelyite from the Black Pine Mine, in Phillipsburg, Montana, was when Leonard Bedale showed us a letter from a miner in Montana who wanted to sell a suite of crystals. He wanted $3,500 for the lot. It was August of 1981, and at the time, it seemed like a lot of money, even for a relatively rare mineral. Jim and Leonard considered purchasing the lot, but they didn't want to do it sight unseen and eventually decided not to do the deal. The miner sold one specimen—the best one—to Gardner Miller in Butte and held onto the rest of the lot.

That December we went to Helena, Montana, for our son Mike's wedding. While we were there, Jim took our new daughter-in-law's father Pete to Drummond, Montana, to see the miner and the veszelyite. Jim and the miner struck a deal, and Jim bought the lot, less the one sold to Gardner Miller, for $2500.

When Jim came back, he laid the specimens out on the bed. There was one miniature that had a piece missing; he picked up a smaller specimen and found that it fit onto the miniature. He repaired the specimen, and it was beautiful. There were a number of nice pieces; we decided to keep the repaired miniature and five thumbnails for our collection. We gave one nice specimen to Leonard Bedale and sold the rest to John Seibel as soon as we got back from the wedding.

This is what Jim wrote on the identification card that went with the veszelyite:

> I bought this lot from a miner, sold most of lot and got money ($2500) back in 2 weeks. The miner collected in about August '81. He claimed he spotted pocket as they were lighting fuses. He collected while partner finished lighting round. Collected with wrench, carried out on hands, mouth, etc. One large xtl [crystal] sold to Gardner Miller. I bought rest, consisting of one superb miniature, 30 fine TN's [thumbnails], 20 lesser, quite a little junk. I kept miniature, 5 TN's; gave one TN to Leonard Bedale, sold rest to J. Seibel for $2500 cost.

It was a pleasant little sidebar to the wedding and proved that no matter what was going on, Jim could find a mineral.

ATACAMITE (Cat. No. T0948), 3.8 cm tall
Moonta Mine, Yorke Peninsula, South Australia, Australia
Purchased from Leonard Bedale in December 1985
Marty Zinn collection; Jeff Scovil photo

This specimen is large for a thumbnail and although we considered it part of our (non-competition) thumbnail collection, it is more properly categorized as a small miniature. Tony Jones brought it into the country via the former Czechoslovakia.

PROUSTITE (Cat. No. T0954), 2.5 cm tall
Oberschlema, Schlema, Erzgebirge, Saxony, Germany
Acquired through a trade/purchase with Allan Young in January 1986
Terry Wallace collection; Jeff Scovil photo

This specimen was probably collected in 1974.

CALCITE with COPPER (Cat. No. T0996), 3.1 cm wide
Kearsarge Mine, Houghton County, Michigan
Purchased with the Leonard Bedale Collection in January 1988
Ralph Clark collection; Jeff Scovil photo

PARADAMITE (Cat. No. T0957), 2.2 cm tall
Ojuela Mine, Mapimí, Durango, Mexico
Purchased from Jim Bleess (ex Dick Bideaux)
Private collection; Jeff Scovil photo

SILVER and ACANTHITE
(Cat. No. T0995), 2.2 cm tall
Arizpe (probably Las Chispas Mine)
Sonora, Mexico
Purchased as part of the Leonard Bedale
collection in January 1988
Terry Wallace collection; Jeff Scovil photo

We did a lot of trading and visiting with Leonard when he was collecting thumbnails; he had a very good collection. Eventually we bought his collection and incorporated most of it into ours.

COPPER (Cat. No. T0997), 2 cm tall
Central Mine, Keweenaw County, Michigan
Purchased as part of the Leonard Bedale
Collection in January 1988
Private collection; Jeff Scovil photo

This beautiful blocky, native copper thumbnail was pictured in George English's 1934 book, *Getting Acquainted with Minerals*. It went from the Carl Bosch collection to the Smithsonian, and then to Dave Wilber. It was part of a group of minerals that Dave Wilber showed Leonard and us in 1981. Leonard bought the specimen.

DIOPTASE (Cat. No. T1007), 2.5 cm tall
Mindouli, Pool Region, Republic of the Congo
Purchased from Tony Jones in June 1988
Ralph Clark collection; Jeff Scovil photo

This was the best piece in Lou Schwartz's collection. Lou had paid Giuseppe Agozzino $2000 for it. Giuseppe later reported that the specimen had been found in 1986. Tony Jones had the specimen, but not realizing its value, he sold it to us for $400.

Rex Harris, John Seibel, and Jim Minette collecting on Rex's red beryl claim in Utah
Dawn Minette photo, 1990

BERYL (Cat. No. T1057), 3 cm tall
Violet Claims, Wah Wah Mountains, Beaver County, Utah
Purchased from Rex Harris in October 1990
Max and Jon Sigerman collection; Jeff Scovil photo

In October 1990, John Seibel, Jim, and I went with Rex Harris to the Violet Claims to collect red beryl. The Red Beryl Mine is on the east side of Utah's Wah Wah Mountains. It looks like a white spot about two thirds of the way up the mountains. The mine is accessed by a northbound turn off of a straight east-west power line road. The turnoff winds around through pinyons and cedars uphill to the mine, which is in a light gray to white volcanic ash formation which has red beryl disseminated sparingly through it.

At the mine, almost no red beryl is visible in the rock. Specimens are embedded in matrix and are found by taking the rocks apart with a hammer and chisel or by using small amounts of explosives. It's a wonder any are found. The crystals are typical of beryl: elongated, hexagonal crystals with flat terminations. They are deep red with clear ends and rhyolite impurities concentrated toward the centers of the crystals.

Jim found a pretty good crystal on matrix; and Rex found (and Jim collected) another good crystal for which we paid Rex $500. After we were done collecting, we went down to Delta and bought a beautiful miniature-sized red hexagonal crystal on matrix at Tina's (Rex's daughter's) jewelry store for $6500, which is pictured on the facing page.

Jim cleaned and trimmed it, and we used it in our thumbnail display. When Rex saw it, he didn't recognize it until Jim pointed out an imperfection on the crystal, which we moved to the back when we mounted it. Seeing that, Rex agreed it was the one that we had bought.

BENITOITE (Cat. No. T1111), 2.5 cm wide
Dallas Gem Mine, San Benito County, California
Purchased from Buzz Gray in June 1993
Max and Jon Sigerman collection; photo ©Harold and Erica Van Pelt

This classic blue, brilliant, complete benitoite triangle was found by Elvis "Buzz" Gray and William "Bill" Forrest in a non-natrolite filled cavity in the ironstone cap rock at the Gem Mine. Bob Gill bought the specimen from Buzz. Later when Buzz was selling Bob's collection, we purchased it. This specimen was pictured in Peter Bancroft's *Gem and Crystal Treasures* (1984) as well as in *American Mineral Treasures* (2008).

LEADHILLITE (Cat. No. T1116), 2.5 cm tall
400 Level, Collins Vein, Mammoth-St. Anthony Mine, Tiger, Pinal County, Arizona
Purchased with the Willard Perkin thumbnail collection in May 1994
Dan and Diana Weinrich collection; Jeff Scovil photo

This superb specimen was our first pick from Willard Perkin's thumbnail collection—a very good old time piece of a rare mineral from Tiger. After Willard's wife died, their son contacted Rock Currier to see if he would like to buy his father's thumbnail collection. It wasn't the sort of thing Rock dealt with, so he told us about the collection and suggested we get in touch with Willard's son. Jim set up an appointment for us to go see the minerals the Saturday before Mother's Day. We arrived at the house and found two well-built, multi-drawered thumbnail cases full of specimens. Jim and I each took a case and started going through it. By the time we were probably four drawers down in our respective cases, Jim looked over at me and I said, Yes!.

We gave Rock a malachite after azurite pseudomorph from Chessy-les-Mines in France, for telling us about the collection.

Right: BENITOITE on NATROLITE
(Cat. No. T1112), 2.6 cm tall
Dallas Gem Mine, San Benito County
California
Purchased from Buzz Gray in June 1993
Jesse La Plante photo

Below: PARAHOPEITE
(Cat. No. T1308), 2.5 cm wide
Broken Hill, Central Province, Kabwe
Zambia
Purchased from Cal Graeber
Jeff Scovil photo

This specimen had previously been in the collection of Frank Knecktal then of Leo and Marion Horensky, the latter of which was being brokered by Cal Graeber when we bought this specimen.

GROSSULAR (Cat. No. T1324), 2.5 cm wide
Jeffrey Mine, Asbestos, Quebéc, Canada
Purchased from Mike Ridding in November 1997
Ralph Clark collection; Jeff Scovil photo

This specimen won 1st place for thumbnails in the 2006 Tucson Gem and Mineral Society show's "Best of Species" competition for Canadian Minerals.

DIOPTASE (Cat. No. T1313), 2 cm tall
Mammoth-St. Anthony Mine, Tiger, Pinal County
Arizona
Purchased from Keith Williams in 1997
Carolyn Manchester collection; Jeff Scovil photo

These two sparkly balls of bright green dioptase are made up of a myriad of needle crystals. This fine old Tiger thumbnail was formerly in the collection of Royal Gould of Ridgecrest, California.

SCHNEIDERHÖHNITE
(Cat. No. T1377), 2.7 cm tall
29 Level, Tsumeb Mine, Otjikoto Region, Namibia
Purchased from Desmond Sacco in 1985
Alex Schauss collection; Jeff Scovil photo

GROSSULAR on DIOPSIDE
(Cat. No. T1419), 2.3 cm tall
Eden Mills, Lamoille County, Vermont
Traded from Roland and Kathy Sherman on
March 15, 2004 (ex Richard Bideaux)
Ralph Clark collection; Jeff Scovil photo

AGUILARITE (Cat. No. T1502), 2.8 cm tall
Guanajuato, Guanajuato, Mexico
Traded from Dave Bunk after 2002
Bill and Carol Smith collection; Jeff Scovil photo

ZEKTZERITE (Cat. No. T1423), 2.1 cm tall
Washington Pass, Okanogan County, Washington
Purchased from C. Carter Rich after Jim died.
Jim and Gail Spann collection; Jeff Scovil photo

THE MISTRESSES

by Paul W. Pohwat

Many serious mineral collectors would love to collect everything that comes their way, if only they had the space to store the pieces and the gelt to ensure that specimens would continue to flow their way. Unfortunately, most collectors lack one or the other, or both, and have to come up with collecting schemes to fit their budgets and living accommodations. Even with a plan, however, many collectors encounter specimens that do not fit their criteria, but they still want them. In spite of reason and whatever discipline collectors may have imposed on themselves, they fall madly, uncontrollably in love with certain specimens that do not fit into one of their specialities. Those who have had this experience, and I count myself among them, eventually amass a subcollection of specimens that are very good and possibly incredibly good, having been selected with the same care and precision that was employed in acquiring specimens for the planned collections. I refer to this suite or subcollection as a "mistress" collection.

The Minette Collection includes specimens that do not fit easily into any of their suites; yet each piece in their mistress collection (catalogued by Jim and Dawn as the "worldwide" collection) is a superb example of the species and would be a welcome addition to almost any collector's cabinet. The beauty and pleasure in the mistresses is that they were largely acquired serendipitously. They are less a representation of the drive that built the other subcollections and more a reflection of their long-term presence in the collecting community and their ability to act quickly on opportunities as they arose. The methods of acquisition tell the story: field collecting, exchanging, and purchasing "sleeper" specimens, which they recognized as bargains.

The comprehensive suites—borates, smithsonite, thumbnails—give the collection its depth and importance; they reflect the Minettes' focus and drive. The mistresses pad the monetary, sentimental, and aesthetic values of the collection and reflect the Minettes' knowledge, patience, savvy, and passion for minerals.

Left: RHODOCHROSITE on QUARTZ (Cat. No. SC002), 12 cm tall, repaired
Collector's Pocket, 2nd Crosscut, Sweet Home Mine, Alma, Park County, Colorado
Collected by Jim Minette and purchased from The Collector's Edge
Jeff Scovil photo

This partially cleaned rhodochrosite on quartz with sphalerite and huebnerite specimen is encrusted with fine-grained silica, as are most of the specimens from this mine. The Collector's Pocket was found on the day that Jim, Wolfgang Mueller, and I were at the mine after the Denver Show. Jim was allowed to recover this specimen after which we purchased it.

AZURITE "Roses" (Cat. No. WW168), to 2 cm wide
3 to 54 Stope Section, Holbrook Mine, Bisbee, Cochise County, Arizona
Purchased in September 2000
Scott Rudolph collection; Jeff Scovil photo

In 1957, one of Jim's professors at the Colorado School of Mines showed him a shoe box filled with azurite "roses" from the world famous copper deposit at Bisbee, Arizona. For forty-two years, the memory of those specimens had haunted Jim until, in 1999, he decided to try to locate that former professor: Ben Parker, Jr. Professor Parker did not live far from where he lived when we went to school; so he was not difficult to find.

Parker, who retired in 1961, had boxed the specimens up then and hadn't looked at them since. We made arrangements to see the collection in conjunction with the 2000 Denver show. Jim and I met the professor, drove to his house in the mountains, and began unpacking large wooden crates filled with minerals, all of which were still wrapped in newspapers from 1961. It was largely a teaching collection and didn't contain many fine specimens. However, as we were going through the crates, we came upon a small round tin and a little wooden box that contained 17 bright, sharp Bisbee azurite "roses." A handwritten label identified them as having come from "3 to 54 Stope Section, Holbrook Mine, Bisbee, Arizona." These specimens appeared to have been carefully collected and matched and were probably together for almost 100 years, as that section of the mine had closed in the early 1900s, and the area where the azurites were found had long been deemed unstable.

Parker said that he had purchased the collection of his predecessor, James Underhill. We therefore assumed that these azurites had belonged to Underhill, who was a prominent surveyor and geologist in Colorado. Doubt has since been cast on that assumption, and I am today unsure who should be credited with preserving the "shoe box azurites."

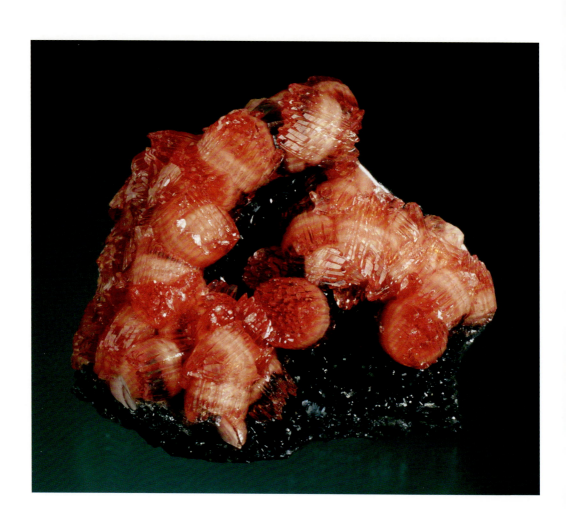

RHODOCHROSITE (Cat. No. WW328), 5.5 cm wide
N'Chwaning Mine, Kalahari Manganese Fields, Northern Cape Province, South Africa
Jim traded borates with Desmond Sacco for this in South Africa.
Marty Zinn collection; Jeff Scovil photo

ALAMOSITE with PLUMBOTSUMITE and MELANOTEKITE (Cat. No. WW332), 6 cm wide
Tsumeb Mine, Otjikoto Region, Namibia
Purchased from Si and Ann Frazier
Jeff Scovil photo

Prosper Williams had this specimen labeled "leadhillite" and offered it for sale for $150 retail, $75 "keystone." Si and Ann Frazier purchased the specimen and had it in their collection for some time. Prosper later came by and saw the specimen in the Frazier's display cabinet and remarked that it had been mislabeled, that the specimen was in fact alamosite—one of the five best to have ever come from Tsumeb.

After some time, quartz collectors Si and Ann decided to sell the specimen. It took them some discussion to settle on an asking price, finally listing it in their pre-Tucson flyer for $4500. When the newsletters went out, Jim Minette was the first of dozens of interested collectors to respond. He asked Ann to hold the specimen until he and Dawn arrived in Tucson, and she agreed. A line had formed at the Fraziers' booth with the hope that their client would not show, but Jim arrived and took the specimen. Dawn returned with a check and the specimen was sold.

MAGNETITE (Cat. No. SC005), 16.2 cm tall
Twin Peaks, Millard County, Utah
Collected by Jim and Dawn Minette in 1990
Dawn Minette-Cooper collection; Jeff Scovil photo

In the summer of 1990, Jim and I took a collecting vacation to Utah. We went to Cedar City, and while we were casting about for a spot to collect, we decided to go to the local college to look at the mineral collection. While we were there, we inquired as to whether anyone knew anything about mineral collecting in the area. Someone directed us to one of the professors in the Geology Department who was absolutely wonderful. Not only did he tell us about collecting localities and minerals, but he also took us out and showed us several places where we could collect magnetite.

I suspect he was a pretty good teacher, and he had a bit of the same attitude Paul Keating had about teaching his students to think. He told us that one of the first field assignments he gave his students was to take them to an area that contained three major magnetite dikes (and many small veinlets) to make a Brunton Compass survey. Poor kids!

The professor gave us quite a bit of his time and took us into the mountains to describe the geology. That evening Jim and I took him and his wife to dinner. The next day, Jim and I went back to the Twin Peaks area (the professor's survey area) to collect magnetite. It was a charming area—lovely, rounded, grassy hills covered with small deciduous and pinyon pine trees. It was very quiet there. We looked across lovely fields toward Cedar City with the wooded hills and mountains beyond. It was one of the most pleasant places I've collected.

There were three large, parallel, black magnetite dikes that outcropped in the hills. The largest and easternmost one was about 3 meters high and about as wide. It stood vertically and was exposed over a distance of about 90 meters. It was mostly massive magnetite with admixed apatite crystals in some areas. Running along the uphill side of the dike was a 15 to 30 centimeter wide magnetite vein. I found it when I was looking over the area. The two outer edges of the vein were fairly straight and parallel, and I noticed there was a jagged line going down the middle of the vein. I wondered if maybe that was the outline of crystal faces and called Jim over to check. He did a bit of excavating and came up with a few crystal specimens. The bases of the specimens were the outsides of the vein; the crystals had formed toward the center of the vein.

In short order Jim had opened a long narrow trench, and we collected several flats of crystals. Jim collected the day's best specimen toward the middle magnetite dike. It was the only specimen I saved when I sold the mineral collection. I saved it because Jim collected it and it reminded me of the good time we had on that trip.

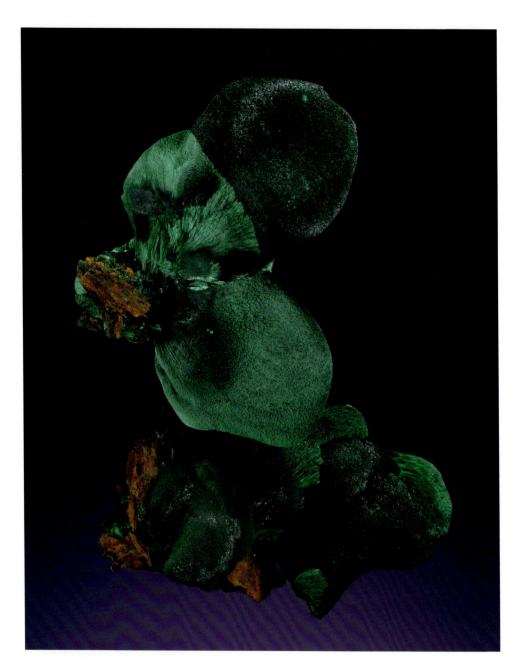

MALACHITE (Cat. No. WW092), 6.5 cm tall
Czar Mine, Bisbee, Cochise County, Arizona
Mark Hay collection; Jeff Scovil photo

CALCITE on CARMINITE (Cat. No. WW347), 5.5 cm tall
Ojuela Mine, Mapimí, Durango, Mexico
Purchased from Moe Leonardi
Tony Potucek collection; Jeff Scovil photo

GALENA with MARCASITE (Cat. No. WW102), 13 cm wide
Galena, Tri-State District, Cherokee County, Kansas
Jeff Scovil photo

FLUORITE with CALCITE (Cat. No. WW104), 23 cm wide
Minerva #1 Mine, Cave-in-Rock, Hardin County, Illinois
Obtained in a trade with Southwest Minerals in 1970.
Jeff Scovil photo

BARITE partially replaced by WOODHOUSEITE (Cat. No. WW123), 6 cm tall
Champion (White Mountain) Mine, White Mountains, Mono County, California
Purchased as part of Ed Swoboda's pseudomorph collection
Smithsonian Institution collection; Jeff Scovil photo

RUTILE (Cat. No. WW212), 13 cm wide
Graves Mountain, Lincoln County, Georgia
Purchased from Rock Currier
Bruce Oreck collection; Jeff Scovil photo

RUTILE with PYROPHYLLITE (Cat. No WW214), 7 cm wide
Champion (White Mountain) Mine, White Mountains, Mono County, California
Purchased from Kristalle
Peter Farquhar collection; Jeff Scovil photo

Ed McDole collected this rutile in the late 1950s; it is one of the largest rutile specimens ever recovered from the Champion Mine. Indeed, Jim collected at Champion for more than forty years. His efforts yielded rutile, woodhouseite, and other species, but he never found a truly good rutile; so when this one was offered, we had to buy it.

QUARTZ on MALACHITE after AZURITE (Cat. No. WW228), 11 cm wide, repaired
Piedmont Mine, Bloody Basin, Yavapai County, Arizona
Les and Paula Presmyk collection; Jeff Scovil photo

We obtained this when we got Ed Swoboda's pseudomorph collection around 1996. It had been collected in the 1950s by Wayne Thompson Sr. and Everett Thompson (Wayne Thompson's uncles) and by Monnie Speck. A large boulder near a fifty-foot shaft showed an interesting seam, and Everett had to blast to obtain the specimens.

ELBAITE, ALBITE and QUARTZ
(Cat. No. WW230)
17 cm wide
repaired and restored

Himalaya Mine, Mesa Grande
San Diego County, California

Purchased from Bill Larson

Marty Zinn collection
Jeff Scovil photo

This specimen was first offered to another collector. He declined, and we jumped at the opportunity to buy it. Bill Larson recently remarked that this was one of the finest matrix pieces ever to have come from the mine.

DYSCRASITE (Cat. No. WW261), 9 cm wide
Príbram, Bohemia, Czech Republic
Jeff Scovil photo

WHEWELLITE (Cat. No. WW278), crystal 2.7 cm tall
Burgk, Saxony, Germany
Jeff Scovil photo

This was one of Jim's favorite specimens. There were two unusually fine examples of this organic mineral in the Minettes' collection.

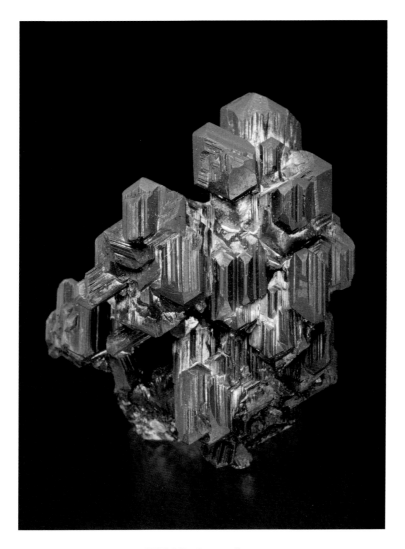

CHALCOCITE (Cat. No. WW289), 4 cm tall
Bristol Copper Mine, Bristol, Hartford County, Connecticut
Gail and Jim Spann collection; Jeff Scovil photo

This old specimen appeared on the covers of *Rocks & Minerals* and *Matrix* (v.5, n.2). It was also pictured in *The Mineralogical Record* (v.32, n.6) and *American Mineral Treasures* (2008).

MALACHITE after GYPSUM (Cat. No. WW300), 9.5 cm tall
Apex Mine, St. George, Washington County, Utah
Purchased with the Ed Swoboda pseudomorph collection
Bob Byers collection; Jeff Scovil photo

CERUSSITE (Cat. No. WW304), 9 cm wide
Tsumeb Mine, Otjikoto Region, Namibia
Purchased from Rock Currier circa 1980
Scott Rudolph collection; John Smolski photo

METATORBERNITE (Cat. No. WW327), 4 cm tall
Musonoi Mine, Katanga (Shaba), Democratic Republic of the Congo (Zaire)
Jim purchased this specimen from Gilbert Gauthier in the 1990s.
Jeff Scovil photo

AXINITE (Cat. No WW329), 3.5 cm tall
New Melones Lake Spillway, Calaveras County, California
Collected by Jim Minette
Jeff Scovil photo

Demetrius Pohl writes,

> The ferroaxinite specimen was one that Jim collected on a Stanford University sponsored collecting trip to the spillway of the New Melones Dam. Jim was also part of a second collecting expedition sponsored by the Smithsonian Institution, where he and others collected some outstanding specimens. The locality was closed to collectors after those two expeditions. I started exchanging minerals by mail from Australia with Jim in 1964 and got to meet him and Dawn for the first time in 1974. We collected together at the Champion Mine, in Boron, and the San Bentito Mountains. We stayed friends until he died.

AZURITE (Cat. No. WW330), 4.5 cm wide
Copper Queen Mine, Bisbee, Cochise County, Arizona (circa 1885)
Paul Harter collection; Jeff Scovil photo

PYROMORPHITE (Cat. No. WW334), 5.5 cm tall, repaired
Bunker Hill Mine, Kellogg, Coeur d'Alene District, Shoshone County, Idaho
Gail and Jim Spann collection; Jeff Scovil photo

This miniature was pictured on the cover of *The Mineralogical Record* (1996) and in the Bunker Hill chapter of *American Mineral Treasures* (2008).

STEPHANITE (Cat. No. WW335), 4.5 cm wide, repaired
Proaño Mine, Fresnillo, Zacatecas, Mexico
Purchased from Dennis Beals in the late 1990s
Jeff Scovil photo

Wendell Wilson liked the specimen so much that he painted a picture of it. The painting is reproduced on page 10 of this book and in *The Mineralogical Record* (v.34, no.6), one of the Mexico issues.

COPPER with CUPRITE and MALACHITE (Cat. No. WW339), 4 cm tall
Tsumeb Mine, Otjikoto Region, Namibia
Purchased from Miriam and Julius Zweibel (Mineral Kingdom)
Scott Rudolph collection; Jeff Scovil photo

PARAVAUXITE on WAVELLITE
(Cat. No. WW351), 2.5 cm tall
Contacto Vein West, Level 411, Llallagua, Bustillos Province,
Potosí Department, Bolivia
ex Mark Bandy collection
Joan Massagué collection; Jeff Scovil photo

NEPTUNITE and BENITOITE (Cat. No. WW605), 13.5 cm wide
Dallas Gem Mine, San Benito County, California
Purchased from Scott Werschky of Miner's Lunchbox in May, 2004 (ex Wayne Sorenson)
Jeff Scovil photo

MALACHITE (Cat. No. WW606), 13.5 cm wide
Luishia Mine, Katanga (formerly Shaba), Democratic Republic of Congo (formerly Zaire)
Purchased from Kristalle at the Denver Show
Lance Cook collection; Jeff Scovil photo

SPRINGFIELD 2002
a tribute to Jim by Dawn Minette-Cooper

Springfield, formally known as the East Coast Gem, Mineral, and Fossil Show, is organized by Marty Zinn. Each year at the show, all 53 of the display cases feature one (or occasionally two or three) collections on a particular theme. The featured exhibitors design and set up their own cases. Marty had been asking Jim and me to exhibit at Springfield, and at the 2001 Tucson show, we agreed to exhibit our collection in 2002.

It is customary for exhibitors to visit the show the preceding year in order to get a feel for the way the show works; so we attended the 2001 show. Les and Paula Presmyk and Evan Jones were exhibiting their Arizona collections that year. We spent a couple of days at the show and met artist Frederick C. Wilda, whom Marty had commissioned to do the artwork for the posters and T-shirts for our show. We gave Fred photographs of several of our specimens. He liked the legrandite "butterfly" (pictured on the cover of this book) the best, but wanted to paint portraits of a couple of the other minerals as well.

Jim and I left the East Coast planning to do the show of August 2002. Little did we know that the MSSC Show in December 2001 would be the last show that Jim and I would attend together. Jim had not been feeling well since mid-November, but we did not know what was wrong. Most of our friends noticed that he was not himself: Much of his time visiting with friends and looking at the latest mineral finds was spent sitting in one or another folding chair. Jim died at home on the twenty-sixth of January 2002, he had been stricken by a fast-growing neuroendocrine cancer. It was a hard time.

While Jim was ill, I had considered cancelling the show, but shortly after he died, I decided that I wanted to exhibit our minerals in Springfield in Jim's memory. I spoke with Dave Bunk (who organizes the Springfield exhibits), and he and Marty agreed to pack the minerals and drive them to Springfield and back. Les and Paula Presmyk offered to help put the displays together—to help in any way that they could.

There is plenty to do in the months following the death of a spouse, and staying busy was therapeutic for me. It wasn't until May that I was able to focus on the project. I had several cases

Left: VIVIANITE (Cat. No. WW262), 10.5 cm tall
Huanuni, Dalence Province, Oruro Department, Bolivia
Richard Jackson collection; Frederick C. Wilda watercolor, 2001

Fred Wilda painted watercolors of three of our specimens: a legrandite thumbnail (the specimen shown on the cover), a cabinet-size Eagle's Nest gold (which had since been broken), and a Bolivian vivianite, reproduced here. Fred's paintings of the vivianite and the legrandite were displayed next to the large case I set up in memory of Jim.

Above: One of the 53 cases at the 2002 James Minette Memorial Exhibit at the East Coast Gem and Mineral Show; John Watson photo

A label for one of the specimens in the exhibit

diagramed before Dave Bunk visited me after the Costa Mesa show in May. We discussed general ideas and came up with a rough plan for the displays. Les Presmyk encouraged me via email, and in June he flew over and spent a day helping me get cases organized.

In the months leading up to the show, I worked nonstop on the exhibit. Les had the blank labels printed. I had been entering the label information into a database so that when the blanks arrived, all I had to do was print them out. I also spent a lot of time getting the minerals prepared: I mounted about 100 thumbnails and another 75 miniatures. In all, some 330 thumbnail specimens and another 380 specimens went to the show. Photos, magazines, posters, and a few mining artifacts also went into the cases.

Dave and Marty arrived with a load of empty boxes on July 26, and the next day, Dave started boxing up the cases of minerals to go to Springfield. Marty and I supplied Dave with boxes and rolls of plastic (the type dry cleaners use), and he did all the packing. Watching the care and efficiency with which Dave packed was quite educational! It took until the middle of the next day for him to finish. Marty and Dave then carefully placed all the boxes in Marty's SUV and took off for Colorado.

I spent the next week finishing my labels and comment cards, and relaxing. It was a good idea to get everything out of the house early. I needed to unwind a bit before heading to the show. My son Mike and his family met me in Hartford on Wednesday, the day before setup. Garth arrived the following day.

On Thursday morning, Mike took me over to the Big E to get the cases ready. Dave was already unloading the boxes of minerals from Marty's van. Les and Paula Presmyk were also there ready to help put the minerals into the cases. After we had all of the minerals in the cases, I added pictures, posters, labels, then checked on the proper placement of the specimens. Before the glass fronts were placed on the cases, Jeff Scovil took pictures of each of them.

The show opened the following day. I spent most of the weekend in the display area visiting with people and showing them the collection. On Friday and Sunday, Les gave a talk/slide show about Jim's life. It was much the same as the memorial he gave at the Tucson show and at our open house, though expanded.

The show was a wonderful experience. I realize now that I was still reeling from Jim's death and I think I could have done a better job had I allowed some more time to pass. But family and friends helped me get through. Jim had died too soon.

Artist Fred Wilda's 2001 watercolor of the Minettes' signature legrandite

WULFENITE (Cat. No. WW177), 17 cm wide, repaired
Glove Mine, near Amado, Santa Cruz County, Arizona
Acquired in trade with the University of Arizona Museum in 1965
Jack and Judy Farnham collection; Jeff Scovil photo

This was, in Jim Minette's opinion, the best piece in the University of Arizona's collection. He traded it for a large borax and probertite specimen, one of the best borates in his collection.

FULL CIRCLE
Dawn Minette-Cooper on selling the collection

A collection should be a living thing, always rising to higher planes. If it stops, it dies.

—British collector Sir John Addis (1914-1983)

Mineral collections aren't just about minerals. They're so much more. They encompass how the minerals were collected—the hunting tales. Like any good hunter, the collector has a tale of how each mineral was found and captured for the collection. And each specimen can be considered a trophy to be admired and shared with friends and other interested souls.

Collections are also a compilation of the history of each specimen: where it came from, and who owned it, before the present owner obtained it—provenance. These bits of information are carefully kept with the specimen so future collectors will know its background.

Jim and I found and collected some of our minerals on collecting trips. We fondly remembered the places where they were found and the circumstances under which we found them. Other specimens can be traced back more than one hundred years, having passed through many loving and often unknown hands before we obtained them. Each mineral has its own story and a memory attached to it.

Our collection is the story of a lifetime fascination with minerals and of the careful and thoughtful effort to obtain and maintain the specimens that we have enjoyed and loved. It is a living entity. Minerals move in and out of the collection, changing its character constantly. After Jim died, I didn't stopped collecting; but I was not giving the collection the attention I should have, and it was beginning to languish. The time had come to sell it.

Jim always wanted to have the collection broken up and sold when he and I died. He wanted other collectors to have the joy of owning the specimens we collected and loved, rather than having them gather dust in the back room of some museum, unseen and unappreciated. He always thought it would be fun to look back from the Great Beyond and see what happened when the collection was sold. He certainly got a show!

I haven't lost my love of minerals or the urge to collect, but I felt the time had come to disburse our collection and start over with a much smaller one. And I wanted to have the pleasure of watching the collection being sold and see things come full circle.

WORKS
referenced and cited

Bancroft, Peter. 1984. *Gem and Crystal Treasures*. Fallbrook, CA: Western Enterprises.

Barnard, Ralph M., and Kistler, Robert B. "Stratigraphic and Structural Evolution of the Kramer Sodium Borate Ore Body, Boron, California." Second Symposium on Salt (1965): 133.

Canfeld, Frederick. 1923. *The Final Disposition of Some American Collections of Minerals*. Dover, NJ: privately published.

Chaucer, Geoffrey. 2003. *The Canterbury Tales*. Trans. Nevill Coghill. London: Penguin Books: 20.

Conklin, Lawrence H. "James Sowerby, His Publications and Collections." *The Mineralogical Record* 26, no. 4 (1995): 89.

Conklin, Lawrence H. 1986. *Notes and Commentaries on Letters to George F. Kunz: Correspondence from Various Sources, including Clarence S. Bement with Facsimiles*. Privately published.

English, George L. 1934. *Getting Acquainted with Minerals*. Rochester, NY: Mineralogical Publishing Co.

Erd, R.C., Morgan, V., and Clark, J.R. "Tunellite, A New Hydrous Strontium Borate from the Kramer Borate District, California." U.S. Geological Survey Professional Paper. (1961): 424-C, 294–297.

Gratacap, Louis Pope. 1912. *A Popular Guide to Minerals*. New York: D. Van Nostrand Company.

Mineralogical Record, The 27, no. 4 (1996): cover.

Mineralogical Record, The 32, no. 7 (2001): 444.

Minette, James W., and Wilber, David P. "Hydroboracite from the Thompson Mine, Death Valley." *The Mineralogical Record* 4, no. 1 (1973): 21.

Minette, James W., and Muehle, Gerhard. "Colemanite from the Thompson Mine." *The Mineralogical Record* 5, no. 2 (1974): 67.

Minette, J.W., "A Notable Probertite Find at Boron, California." *The Mineralogical Record* 19, no. 5 (1988): 315.

Morgan, Vincent, and Erd, Richard C. "Minerals of the Kramer Borate District, California." Mineral Information Service: A Publication of the California Division of Mines and Geology 22, no. 9 (1969): 151.

Romé de Lisle, Jean Baptiste Louis. 1783. Cristallographie: ou Description des Formes Propres a Tous Les Corps Du Regne Minéral, Dans L'état de Combinaison Saline, Pierreuse ou Métallique, Avec Figures & Tableaux Synopitques de Tous les Cristaux Connus. Paris: Imprimerie de Monsieur.

Staebler, Gloria A., and Wilson, Wendell E. 2008. *American Mineral Treasures*. East Hampton, CT: Lithographie, LLC.

Whistler, D.P. "A New Hemmingfordian (Middle Miocene) Mammalian Fauna from Boron, California, and its Stratigraphic Implications Within the Western Mojave Desert." Program Abstracts, Fifth Annual Graduate Symposium in the Geological Sciences (1965).

Wilson, Wendell. "The History of Mineral Collecting 1530-1799." *The Mineralogical Record* 25, no. 6 (1994): 25.

Wilson, Wendell. "The History of Mineral Collecting 1530-1799." *The Mineralogical Record* 25, no. 6 (1994): 57.

INDEX
of species and localities

Acanthite, **144**

Aguilarite, **156**

Alamosite, 164, **165**

Albite, **182-183**

Atacamite, **140**

Aurichalcite, **135**

Australia
    New South Wales, 127, 130, 133
    South Australia, 140

Axinite-(Fe), **194**, 195

Azurite, **160**, 161, **180**, 181, 196, **197**

Barite, 174, **175**

Benitoite, 148, **149**, **151**, 206, **207**

Beryl, 146, **147**

Bolivia
    Oruro Department, 211
    Potosí Department, 130, 205

Borax, 42, **43**

Calcite, **48**, 49, 50, **51**, 52, **53**, **54**, 55, 56, **57**, **58-59**, 142, **169**, 172, **173**

Canada, Quebéc, 152

Carminite, **169**

Celestine, 68, **69**, 76, **77**

Cerussite, 82, **83**, 92, **93**, 190, **191**

Chalcocite, **187**

Colemanite, **48**, 49, **50**, 51, 52, **53**, **54**, 55, 56, **57**, 60, **61**, 64, **65**, 68, **69**, 70, **71**, **72**, 76, 77

Copper, **142**, **144**, 202, **203**

Coronadite, **127**

Cuprite, 202, **203**

Czech Republic, Bohemia, 185

Democratic Republic of Congo (formerly Zaire), 145, 192, 208

Diopside, **155**

Dioptase, **145**, **153**

Dyscrasite, **184**, 185

Elbaite, **6**, **182-183**

Fluorite, 172, **173**

Galena, **170**, 171

Germany, Saxony, 141, 186

Goethite, 80, **81**, 100, **101**

Gold, **135**

Grossular, **152**, **155**

Gypsum, **188**, 189

Hessite, **135**

Hydroboracite, 66, **67**

Inderite, 44, **45**

Inyoite, 64, **65**

Italy, Sardinia, 120

Kurnakovite, 44, **45**

Leadhillite, **150**

Legrandite, **cover**, iv, **213**

Magnetite, 166, **167**

Malachite, **168**, **180**, 181, **188**, 189, 202, **203**, 208, **209**

Marcasite, **170**, 171

Melanotekite, 164, **165**

Metatorbernite, 192, **193**

Mexico
  Durango, **cover**, iv, 143, 169
  Guanajuato, 156
  Sonora, 144
  Zacatecas, 5, 200

Meyerhofferite, 74, **75**

Morocco, 126, 128

Namibia
  Otjikoto (Tsumeb), 92, 94, 97, 98, 99, 100, 102, 104, 106, 108, 134, 154, 164, 190, 202
  Otjozonjupa (Berg Aukas), 110, 113, 114, 117

Natrolite, **151**

Neptunite, **132**, 206, **207**

Orpiment, 52, **53**

Paradamite, **143**

Parahopeite, **116**, **151**

Paramelaconite, 136, **137**

Pararealgar, 60, **61**

Paravauxite, **204**, 205

Phosphophyllite, **130**

Plumbotsumite, 164, **165**

Probertite, **62**, 63

Proustite, **141**

Pyromorphite, 198, **199**

Pyrophyllite, **178**, 179

Pyroxmangite, **133**

Quartz, **180**, 181, **182-183**

Rhodochrosite, **158**, 159, **162**, 163

Rhodonite, **130**

Romania, 135

Rosasite, **99**

Rutile, **176-177**, **178**, 179

Scheiderhöhnite, **154**

Scorodite, **134**

Silver, **144**

Smithsonite, 79, **80**, 81, **82**, 83, 84, **85**, 86, **87**, 88, **89**, **90-91**, 92, **93**, 94, **95**, **96-97**, **98**, **99**, **100**, **101**, 102, **103**, 104, **105**, 106, **107**, 108, **109**, **110**, 111, **112**, 113, **114-115**, **116**, **117**, 118, **119**, 120, **121**, 122, 123, 124, **125**, **126**, **127**, **128**, **129**, **135**

Stephanite, **4**, 200, **201**

South Africa, Northern Cape, 163

Tennantite, 102, **103**

Tincalconite, 42, **43**

Tunellite, 46, **47**

Ulexite, 40, **41**, 46, **47**, **54**, 55, **58-59**

United States
  Arizona, 136, 150, 153, 161, 168, 181, 196, 214
  Arkansas, 122, 124
  California, **27**, **29**, **30**, 31-33, **36**, 37, **38** (map), 39, 40, **42**, 44, 46, 49, 50, 52, 55, 56, 59, 60, 62, 64, 66, 68, 70, 72, **73**, 74, **76**, 118, 132, 134, 148, 151, 174, 179, 182, 195, 206
  Colorado, 21, 159
  Connecticut, 187
  Georgia, 176
  Idaho, 198
  Illinois, 172
  Kansas, 171
  Michigan, 142, 144
  Montana, 138
  New Mexico, 81, **83**, 84, 86, 88, 90, 135
  Utah, 146, 166, 189
  Vermont, 155
  Washington, 157

Veszelyite, 138, **139**

Viviante, **210**, 211

Wavellite, **204**, 205

Whewellite, 186

Willemite, **114-115**, **117**

Woodhouseite, **134**, 174, **175**

Wulfenite, **214**

Zambia, 116, 129, 151

Zektzerite, 157